HUMAN SERVICE
PLANNING AND EVALUATION
FOR HARD TIMES

HUMAN SERVICE PLANNING AND EVALUATION FOR HARD TIMES

By

ALAN BOOTH, Ph.D.

Professor, Sociology Department
University of Nebraska-Lincoln
Lincoln, Nebraska

and

DOUGLAS HIGGINS, M.A.

Executive Director
United Way of Lincoln and Lancaster County
Lincoln, Nebraska

CHARLES C THOMAS • PUBLISHER
Springfield • Illinois • U.S.A.

Published and Distributed Throughout the World by
CHARLES C THOMAS • PUBLISHER
2600 South First Street
Springfield, Illinois 62717

© *1984 by* CHARLES C THOMAS • PUBLISHER
ISBN 0-398-04979-3
Library of Congress Catalog Card Number: 83 24278

With THOMAS BOOKS *careful attention is given to all details of manufacturing
and design. It is the Publisher's desire to present books that are satisfactory as to
their physical qualities and artistic possibilities and appropriate for their
particular use.* THOMAS BOOKS *will be true to those laws of quality that
assure a good name and good will.*

Library of Congress Cataloging in Publication Data

Booth, Alan, 1935—
    Human service planning and evaluation for hard times.

    Bibliography: p.
    Includes index.
    1. Social service—United States—Planning. 2. Social service—United States—Evalua-
tion. 3. Social service—United States—Finance. 4. Local finance—United States.
I. Higgens, Douglas. II. Title.
HV95.B65   1984   361.2'5'0973   83—24278
ISBN 0—398—04979—3

Printed in the United States of America
PS-R-3

PREFACE

In recent years, human services have faced cutbacks in funding from federal, state, and local government sources, an economic recession, and an increase in demand for services from those affected by the recession. While the recession is becoming less severe, there is no evidence that government spending is likely to increase in the near future. It is in times of resource scarcity that planning and evaluation become particularly critical. Agency executives look for ways to cut expenses and, as a way to retain present levels of funding, to show that their programs are effective and needed. United Way allocation teams, county human service coordinators, elected officials, foundation executives, and others responsible for allocating resources want priorities established, indicators of program effectiveness devised, and criteria to guide their funding decisions developed. While at the federal and state level, planning and evaluation information prepared by experts is often available, at the local level such guidelines rarely exist, and when they do they are often incomplete or of poor quality. The simple application of federal or state guidelines is not practical, because they are expensive to use, geared to large organizations, and demand technical skills often not available at the local level.

This book is designed for human service agency executives and public and private funding organization administrators at the local level. Step-by-step procedures are set forth for cutback planning and management, assessing program effectiveness, monitoring client outcomes, allocating resources across a variety of agencies, evaluating agencies, and establishing priorities. The guidelines rest on up-to-date methods of planning and evaluation that have been tested at the local level. The book is written for individuals who have had no formal training in planning and evaluation as well as those who have had some course work. The guidelines are inexpensive and simple to implement.

In preparing guidelines for agency executives and funding organization administrators in the same book, the writer recognizes the goal these individuals share (to provide high quality services to those in need), and the close working relationship needed to achieve that goal. The differences are also taken into account. Agency executives are more interested in maximizing access to resources, while funding administrators are more concerned with a balanced distribution of funds among competing agencies and accountability to taxpayers and donors. An understanding of how each group may better achieve its goals will help both in doing a more effective job.

The first three chapters are directed primarily toward human service agency executives and deal with cutback planning and management, assessing program effectiveness, and monitoring the impact of the program on clients. The next three chapters, directed primarily to funding organization administrators, focus on procedures for allocating resources. The first of the three deals with the overall process, while the remaining two focus on two specific aspects of the process, program evaluation and establishing priorities. While each chapter has a primary audience (agency executives or funding organization administrators), there is a section devoted to the other reader which contains suggestions as to how they can make use of and facilitate the operations and procedures recommended. The final chapter suggests ways of integrating private and public human service planning and evaluation at the local level. It is based on the development of the only fully intergrated human service planning operation at the metropolitan level in the country. It has been operating smoothly since 1979 and has become a model for other communities.

ACKNOWLEDGMENTS

To write on a topic as broad as human service planning and evaluation, help and advice from a great number of people is needed. We have learned much from clients, agency executives, public officials, and volunteers. We could easily name more than 100 people to whom we are deeply indebted. Special thanks go to Bob Clark, Cheryl Naber, Teri Tuma, Doug Wagner, and Susan Welch for the privilege of learning from them.

CONTENTS

HUMAN SERVICE
PLANNING AND EVALUATION
FOR HARD TIMES

Chapter 1

COPING WITH DECLINING HUMAN SERVICE RESOURCES: GUIDELINES FOR AGENCY EXECUTIVES

INTRODUCTION

Cutbacks in tax dollars, coupled with a recession bred reluctance to make donations, have placed many human service agencies in the position of responding to pressures to meet increasing or constant demands with fewer resources. One strategy for relief is to raise revenues from new sources or extract additional funds from old sources. Other strategies include cutting expenses and making more efficient use of existing resources. Whether one or a combination of strategies is used, a plan should guide the process. This chapter begins by describing an effective way to formulate a plan. Ways of raising revenue are considered, along with the income generating potential of each strategy. General guidelines for cutting expenses are proposed, as are specific methods for reducing expenditures. The hazards involved in implementing each strategy are reviewed. The chapter concludes with a case study of an agency that developed what the authors consider a model response to a major reduction in revenue.

LONG- OR SHORT-TERM PLANNING

While a number of indicators suggest that the recession is becoming less severe, there is disagreement about the extent and length of recovery that can be anticipated. Even if economic recovery is at hand, the prospect for growth in the human service sector remains bleak. There is no evidence that the mood of the voters to reduce spending is abating, and spending lids are likely to be with us for some time. For these reasons, it is recommended that human service agencies develop a long-term plan (three to five years) for coping with limited or decreasing resources. As will be shown later (under the topic Principles of Cutting Expenses), annual plans often have long term consequences that interfere with the agency's ability to provide quality service.

SETTING PRIORITIES

Priorities are at the root of a plan to cope with economic decline. Once established, they guide decisions on raising revenue, cutting expenses, and numerous other issues that arise in the management of a human service agency. Setting priorities simply means deciding which services are to receive more resources, which are to receive less, and ranking the services accordingly. The answers to three questions serve as the basis for assigning rankings:

1. Which services do clients need the most?

   Perhaps they are the services that are designed for the clients with the most severe problems, or services that the clients cannot receive from another source.

2. What does the agency do best?

   It is a sound strategy to continue to provide the services for which the staff has the most training and experience. These are probably the services that constitute the largest part of the agency's workload, and the services that are tendered most efficiently.

3. Which services generate the greatest revenue now and are likely to continue to do so in the future?

   Services that generate little income (either through client fees, reimbursements, grants, or contracts) should have lower priority, because they do the least to defray expenses.

To set priorities, detailed information on all three questions should be gathered for each service. Caseload records yield information on types of clients and their problems as well as the demand for various types of services. Financial records, combined with caseload data, provide information on the income and expenses per unit of service. Questionnaire data from clientele will yield information on the most urgent needs from the consumer's point of view and strategies they might use if the service were no longer available, or available at a higher fee. Support, professional and administrative staff are excellent sources of information for all three questions. The information should be assembled and summarized for use in assigning priorities.

Gathering information from all staff levels (support, professional, and administrative) as well as clients is the first step to developing a broad base of support for the financial plan. The second step is involving a cross section of people (those involved in providing direct service, as well as administrators) in establishing the priorities. Setting priorities should not be the task of one person or that of an executive committee. The task is unusual and complex, and there is much at stake. If the agency is small, the entire staff could take part; or a special committee could be formed that has representation from various aspects of the agency's operation. Board support is, of course, essential. Whether it should be involved in these preliminary steps or later depends on the working relationship between agency staff and members of the board.

Early in the priority setting process, it is necessary to devise a list of services that people agree represent the agency's mission. One or two people may draft a list, which is then circulated among those who are going to be assigning priorities for additions and revisions. Agreement may require some deliberation and compromise, because people may differ in their views as to what constitutes a service.

Distribute the information on each service and have people in the prioity-setting group rank each service independently without consulting others. They might assign rankings as follows: highest prioity, high priority, moderate priority, low priority, lowest priority. People should assign their rankings so that services are distributed across all priority levels. To assign a service to "lowest priority" does not mean it is an unimportant service. It means that relative to other services offered, the consequences of dropping the service are less severe.

After judgments are made independently, the priority-setting group should meet and consider each service in turn. At the meeting, the rankings of each member should be revealed. Unless there is complete agreement, the distribution of ratings should be discussed: individuals may justify their judgments with concrete illustrations and information, balancing such factors as client need with revenue generated. After an exchange of views, members should rank the services again. If there is still little consensus, the process of discussing and ranking should be repeated. The object is to reach a clear consensus rather than arriving at a priority for a given service by a vote or two. To reach consensus, it may be necessary to redefine the service, subdividing it further or combining it with another. Or, it may be necessary to move on to another service and return to the one causing difficulty after completing the work on other services.

After all of the services have been assigned priority ratings, the group should look at the overall rankings to make sure (1) the services have priority assignments that are consistent with one another, that is, the overall set of priorities makes sense, and (2) that there are services in each priority category. If adjustments need to be made, the group should continue working until the problems are resolved. The group should keep in mind that the product is not cast in stone; and, if after some use it is apparent it is not working, revisions can be made. Once the priorities are completed, they should be widely distributed so that all staff, volunteers, and board members know what they are, and that they will be used in agency decision making.

Once priorities are established, the responsibility for incorporating them into a specific plan shifts to the people that ordinarily make decisions about the organization—the executive director, other officers, executive committee, and board. To have the priority setting group or others involved in cutback decisions would be divisive and demoralizing. Also, the priority-setting group may not be willing to make decisions that are unpleasant in the immediate future, but that will benefit the agency over the long haul.

PROJECTING REVENUE AND EXPENSES

A plan requires estimates of future income and expenses. These are often hard to make because legislative decisions vary from year to year, and often funding is not known until the last minute. Nevertheless, it is possible to make relatively reliable estimates using a few simple guidelines. First, it is safe to assume that, with few exceptions, tax dollars for human services are going to decline or remain the same for the planning period. Second, granting and contracting agencies are probably going to act in the future as they have in the recent past. Third, economic recovery is going to be slow, so that for the planning period little change can be expected that is going to affect appreciably the client population in a positive way. Fourth, the competition for private dollars is keen; therefore, the chances of successfully tapping such funds are less than before. By relying on these assumptions and using information from the recent past, along with information obtained from insiders at funding agencies, fairly reliable estimates can be made about the percent increase or decrease in revenues that can be expected over the planning period.

For sources that have behaved erratically in the past, an average estimate and a worst estimate can be made. By worst, we don't mean the worst possible case, but one having a reasonable likelihood of occurring. This may mean that two plans need to be constructed. One is based on a modest change, and the other is based on adverse funding conditions. Begin with the modest change plan and switch to the adverse conditions plan if worst fears come to pass.

Estimating expenses involves the same strategy; making estimates based on what has happened in the recent past. If supplies have gone up an average of 7 percent each year, then use that figure to project expenses for the planning period. Contact suppliers to get their estimates as well. Comparison of expenses over the planning period with anticipated revenues will give some indication of the depth of the cuts that will be needed and the amount of revenue that would need to be raised to avoid cuts. This procedure is, of course, a good budgeting practice anytime.

Estimates of the extent to which projected revenues are below expenses indicate the magnitude of the agency's problem. While it is possible that one could raise sufficient revenue to cover the projected deficit, it is unlikely. Thus, cuts can be anticipated. Priorities are a guide to raising revenue as well as to cutting expenses as the following discussion indicates. While it is not always possible to follow priorities explicitly, a good part of the decision making should be guided by them.

RAISING REVENUE

In the paragraphs that follow, the authors attempt to present a balanced assessment of the fund raising potential of each method. In presenting the pros and cons, they do not intend to discourage agencies from starting fund raising initiatives. They only wish to stress the need for careful planning before embarking on fund raising ventures.

The following are some of the most frequently used methods of raising revenue.

REGENERATIVE FUNDING. This is a procedure whereby the agency goes into business for itself by starting a retail outlet, selling a service, or manufacturing a product. Some agencies, such as Goodwill, have been extraordinarily successful; but these are the exceptions. To date, there are very few human service agencies that have been able to raise significant funds through regenerative funding. Those agencies which have been successful are very large, with budgets in the millions, and have had access to large amounts of capital, for that is what it takes to get a business started and to operate it long enough (three years) to realize a profit. Even if the business survives (80% do not), the return is small. The majority of businesses return a profit of 3 to 7 percent. That means the enterprise needs to have $500,000 in sales to generate $25,000 of profit which can be used to provide human services. Moreover, the types of products a human service agency could offer, such as training, management, and counseling are already offered by the private sector. Those who have been in business for a number of years would offer strong competition to a newcomer and thereby reduce the chances of success even further. Thus, we do not recommend regenerative funding as a viable option for most human service agencies. Those who wish to pursue it further should contact other agencies in their community who have started regenerative funding projects to further assess their own potential for success and to get ideas on how to get started. A number of cities have started seed grant programs in regenerative funding for nonprofit organizations. A call to the mayor's office would reveal whether such a project is under way in your community.

SALES, RAFFLES, MARATHONS, MEMBERSHIP DRIVES, AND OTHER SOURCES. While such events do raise money, they require a large and dedicated group of volunteers or clients to make them a success. Even then, the money raised is in small amounts. If the agency does not have a cadre of volunteers or clients, such events are going to draw heavily on staff time, which detracts from the provision of services. If staff time is already in short supply because of cutbacks, the problem is compounded. Ready access to a large market (a favorable location, an affluent clientele or set of volunteers) is also an important consideration. If clients or volunteers are not experienced at raising funds, leadership training is needed to acquire the expertise needed to do an effective job. One final note: Tax-supported agencies do not have the legal authority to raise funds, and private agencies risk losing their tax-exempt status by raising funds in this way. One solution for tax-supported agencies is to establish a public foundation that can carry out the fund raising activities and channel the money to the agency. Contact the city attorney in your community for further information on establishing such a foundation.

FOUNDATIONS. Fondations are now being bombarded with applications so the competition for funds is stiff. While the *Foundation Directory* will list many national and local foundations with areas of interest that include human services, many already have their funds committed and are not looking for new outlets. Watch the papers for announcements of awards that are made locally by foundations. These are your better prospects. Most foundations are not interested in making long-term commitments. Moreover, they are seldom interested in funding ongoing programs. The project most likely to receive funding is something new that can be funded in one shot; start-up funds for a new program or a capital expenditure of some kind.

In times of economic cutback, it is risky to start a new program for which alternative sources of funds are going to have to be found when foundation money runs out. It is perhaps more reasonable to request that funds be shifted from an old, unproductive program to a new, productive one. Or, it may be sound to apply for funds to buy a building if you are leasing space, to

purchase equipment that you ordinarily rent, or to replace
equipment that is costing a lot to maintain because of its age or
condition. Unless the equipment or space is somehow closely
linked to direct service, the application will probably not have
enough appeal to receive an award. To try to replace the office
copier through a foundation grant is probably not worth the
effort. Consulting firms that assist in preparing grant applications have sometimes been used to good advantage.

INCREASING REVENUE FROM CURRENT SOURCES. Except for
emergency situations (the furnace quits, the roof begins leaking, a
vital piece of equipment breaks), it is unlikely that agencies are
going to get much of an increase for existing programs. Developing a new program is an option; but as noted previously, offering a
new service may not solve the problem of limited resources but
may, in fact, make it worse. If the new service is one that is quite
likely to grow so that there will be new state or federal tax dollars
available in the near future, the risk may be worth it. A
demonstration program in place may have an advantage in
acquiring new funds.

CLIENT FEES. Client Fees are a significant source of funds for
some human service agencies. Fees can be raised as a means to
generate revenue. To raise fees above what similar agencies are
charging, however, will drive clients away and reduce revenue. It
is worthwhile to regularly monitor the fee schedules of agencies
providing similar services and to raise fees to bring them into line
with other agencies. Some agencies lose significant revenue
because they are ineffective in collecting the fees they charge.
Aggressive and systematic efforts to collect from individuals in
arrears is worth the effort. Deposits, payment at the time service is
rendered, or fees for delinquent payments may be used to increase
this source of revenue.

CONTRACTING SERVICES TO OTHER NONPROFIT AND PUBLIC
AGENCIES. Occasionally it may be possible to offer services to
other agencies as a way of maintaining the integrity of the
organization. While this does not directly contribute revenue to
meet expenses, it may do so indirectly. When facing cutbacks in
staff, the provision of services to other agencies allows one to
maintain the full range of services needed by the clients. Letting
staff go and purchasing specialized professional services on a part-

time basis might be more costly. Alternatively, clients would have to rely on professionals whose specialty was not directly related to the problem. Contracting with other agencies allows the agency to maintain the highly trained and experienced staff until the fiscal crisis eases. While not all human service agencies have services in demand by other public or nonprofit organizations, for those that do, this may represent a revenue generating option worth exploring.

SUGAR DADDIES AND SUCH. Most human service executives dream of the private benefactor who would be willing to make a large donation each year or who would direct the earnings from an investment or patent to the agency. Another fantasy is the business that is willing to sponsor an agency and donate services, facilities, and equipment on a large scale. These things occur often enough to keep the dream alive but not frequently enough to warrant investing a lot of time searching for a sugar daddy. Businesses already make substantial contributions of money and employee time to human service agencies through the United Way, and the likelihood of further generosity, especially when many businesses are suffering, is remote except for occasional small, one-time contributions.

By reviewing the potential sources of revenue, not only does the agency executive gain a clear understanding of the revenue that can be expected over the planning period, but that executive is in a position to put into place a plan to begin raising that income.

PRINCIPLES IN CUTTING EXPENSES

There are four general guidelines to cutting expenses that deserve consideration before getting into specifics.

ONE OR TWO CUTS, RATHER THAN MANY. Making a number of small cuts every few months is to be avoided. Research on this matter is quite clear. Frequent small cuts lower employee morale and decrease worker productivity (cf. Greenhalgh and McKensie, 1980). It is far better to estimate the size of the total cut that will be needed over a period of two or three years and then make it all at one time. This does not mean that some things cannot be reduced in several steps to give staff and clients time to adjust, but the entire plan for cutting should be announced at one time so that uncertainty is minimized and that all concerned know exactly what will occur and when.

WHICH CLIENTS TO SERVE AND WHICH TO CUT. Priorities are the primary guide in deciding which clients are to receive full service and which ones are to receive no service or reduced service. Client service decisions have a direct bearing on the specific categories of cuts described below. At times it may be possible to offer reduced services to low-priority clients, and we strongly recommend it. For example, referral services may be offered to low-priority clients; or an intake interview, perhaps by phone, might be conducted so that the client can be given some suggestions as to how he or she might relieve the problem without professional help. Clients are still receiving professional help, but at a reduced level. Offering limited service maintains the integrity of the program while at the same time meeting the financial exigency.

ACROSS THE BOARD VERSUS TARGETED CUTS. A frequent response to declining revenues and rising costs is to freeze salaries, work fewer hours, postpone hiring, and cut all other expenses by some fixed percent for the year. This may be a solution if all that is needed is a quick fix; that is, when the shortfall is clearly temporary and a new infusion of funds is definitely in the works for the following year.

Most human service agencies are not fortunate enough to be facing a short-term problem. In the face of continuing poor financial prospects, the across-the-board cut is a poor strategy. It simply delays having to make hard decisions and leads to very serious problems. Staff with the greatest experience and talent will leave, as they can do better in agencies making targeted cuts or in some other type of organization. Moreover, those who are doing the best work see individuals who are not pulling their weight getting the same rewards (salaries as well as program funds) as themselves; this leads to low morale and declining productivity. Agencies can least afford declining morale and productivity when they are trying to maintain quality service in the face of resource shortfalls.

Targeted cuts are recommended as the best solution to maintaining a quality service in times of economic decline. Research (cf. Levine, 1983) has shown that there is one case when "sharing the pain" (across-the-board cuts) sometimes works, and that is when the organization is very small (seven people or less). In such instances an *esprit de corps* sometimes develops that gets them through long periods of deprivation. In larger groups such solidarity never seems to emerge.

CUTTING DEEP ENOUGH. It is tempting to cut just enough to get by each year and not cut deep enough to generate additional resources to channel into high-priority areas. We believe it is important to cut deep enough to reward valued employees with solid merit increases and fringe benefits and to allocate additional support services (new staff and other resources) to especially productive subunits so that they can increase their effectiveness even further. Persons and units that are particularly efficient should also be rewarded. This will have long-term payoffs in that the agency will appear more attractive to funding sources and maximize productivity in times of economic decline.

SPECIFIC CUTS

The following paragraphs comment on a number of specific ways to cut expenses. Some agencies will have had to implement all or most of the suggested cuts. Others, however, are just beginning to make deep cuts, and the suggestions that follow comprise a brief inventory of areas to consider.

TERMINATING PERSONNEL. One of the most painful experiences agency executives ever face is letting an employee go who has been doing a satisfactory job; and because the largest category of expense in operating a human service agency is personnel, such decisions must be faced frequently. Selection of employees for termination should be guided by whether the individual is working in a high-priority service area. Other important criteria are productivity, experience, and years employed. Information on these criteria must be collected in a complete and systematic way and used to formulate balanced judgements. Once a judgment is reached, every effort should be made to help the employee make the transition. This may mean arranging for early retirement, a healthy allotment of severance pay, employing the person half-time up to a year or until he or she finds another job, paying for and arranging for retraining or counseling, and beating the bushes for a job in another agency. Years of satisfactory service must be rewarded by more than the offer of letters of reference and a few weeks notice. Sometimes termination can be avoided through attrition. If attrition occurs in a high-priority area, it may be possible to retrain a valued employee in a low-priority area and move him or her into the vacant position. Finally, it is important to have a policy for evaluating positions that become available through attrition to determine whether the work can be done by a part-time individual, paraprofessional, or other person that would result in cutting expenses.

PARAPROFESSIONALS.   The use of lower-salaried paraprofessionals is a viable way to reduce expenses in many areas. Paraprofessionals may be recruited from support staff or college student interns, as well as those formally trained as paraprofessionals. In many cases, the agency may have to do much of the training themselves. It is important to realize that many professionals may feel threatened by the use of paraprofessional staff, so that plenty of ground work must be laid out before their introduction. One way of doing this is to involve the professional staff in identifying tasks the paraprofessional can do and defining the supervision that is necessary to insure successful use of such individuals.

VOLUNTEERS.   The use of volunteers is an excellent way to cut expenses. Unfortunately, from the agency perspective, with the tremendous increase in the number of women who have joined the labor force, the number of adult volunteers has declined. There has been, however, an increase in the number of high school and college-age volunteers. Nevertheless, the demand for volunteers at a United Way's Volunteer Center in one Midwestern city is three times the number they can place. One should not give up trying, however. One out of three chances is not bad. Also, if appropriate, one should explore the possibility of getting retired persons through the Retired Senior Volunteer Program or the Service Corps of Retired Executives found in many communities.

MICROCOMPUTERS.   There has been a good deal of interest in using microcomputers for bookkeeping, maintaining mailing lists, work processing, and drafting budgets. Embarking on such a project must be done with great care and planning. One agency with which we are familiar purchased a microcomputer, and the entire project took nearly three years. Selecting hardware and software (programs), training staff, obtaining funds, and making the system operational takes considerable time and attention. The agency was able to eliminate a half-time position, but the savings only amounted to $1,200 per year because the operating cost includes making payments on a loan used to purchase the equipment. The agency has a number of hours each day that it is willing to rent to other agencies at seven dollars per hour. Because of relatively high start-up costs, agencies should consider renting time on existing equipment.

STRETCHING THE OPERATING BUDGET. Frequently, costs can be cut by careful monitoring and control of routine expenses. While each item in itself may not represent much of a savings, over an extended period it can mean hundreds or even thousands of dollars. Ways of saving paper include using the back of paper for writing drafts and notes to staff, writing brief replies on the bottom of the letter and returning it to the sender, making only the number of copies needed and no extras, having people share copies at meetings, and routing materials rather than sending copies to everyone. Avoid mailing materials that can, with a little forethought, be handed out at meetings. Plan far enough ahead so that materials can be mailed third class instead of first class. Private mail services that help agencies take advantage of bulk rates have been shown to generate significant savings. These and other procedures can make a significant dent in office expenses.

SHARING SERVICES AND CONSULTANTS WITH OTHER AGENCIES. It may be possible to cut expenses by sharing services with other agencies. When bringing in a consultant to train staff or review a program, see if he or she can be used in another agency and thereby split the cost. There are a number of services that might be obtained at a better price if several agencies went together and guaranteed a certain volume of work. Collection agencies, auditing firms, bookkeepers, copying or printing services, data processing organizations, secretarial firms, and telephone answering services might be willing to consider such arrangements.

BUYING IN QUANTITY. Buying a year's supply is cheaper than buying material for a few months. Agencies might pool their needs to get a better price on all sorts of office supplies and equipment, liability insurance, or auto insurance. It would require considerable planning and perhaps some compromises on the quality or quantity of a particular item, but the savings could be considerable.

BENEFIT PACKAGES. United Way already has a group health insurance plan in which its affiliates can take part. Nonaffiliates might want to try to organize a similar plan. Life or disability insurance may represent another employee benefit that could be purchased by a group of agencies.

SHARING EMPLOYEES. There are a number of types of employees who could be employed by more than one agency or employed in one agency but used in several with participating agencies paying back in kind or other services. Instructors, counselors, secretaries, clerks, and bookkeepers are such individuals. By pooling, agencies could accomodate variable demands without having to rely on expensive outside services, employ a full-time person who would be underutilized, overwork existing staff, or pay staff at high overtime rates.

CASE STUDY OF CUTBACK

Legal Services of Southeast Nebraska (LSSN) provides legal services to low-income individuals on civil matters. The agency had its 1981 budget cut by 19 percent because of a cutback in federal funds. Legal Services of Southeast Nebraska's Executive Director decided that the only way to handle a cut of such magnitude was to reduce the caseload and terminate staff. Before doing so, priorities were established. Fifty clients were given questionnaires to fill out when they came to the office. Existing caseload was examined to get a clear idea of the nature of the demand. On the basis of this information, a list of priorities was prepared and given to a priority setting committee as something from which to begin their deliberations. The Committee, consisting of three attorneys, one paralegal, and two support staff, was charged with deciding which types of clients would continue to be taken and which would only receive information and referral services. After making ratings and deliberating about them, the Committee came to agreement on a set of priorities. The Board of Directors reviewed the proposed priorities and approved them.

Five staff (professionals and nonprofessionals) were terminated. The decision was made by the Executive Director, who took into account such things as whether staff members' specialties were in a high-priority area or not, productivity, and length of association with LSSN.

In addition, LSSN contracted with two other public agencies that had demands for more services than they could handle. These contracts allowed LSSN to retain the full complement of expertise needed to service their clients and maintain the integrity of the organization until their budget grows to the point where they can again offer more services.

In addition, LSSN was very active in helping the Nebraska Bar Association to organize a volunteer service. Clients who could not be served by LSSN can now be directed to attorneys who serve the clients at little or no cost.

RECOMMENDATIONS FOR FUNDING ORGANIZATION ADMINISTRATORS

In cutting human service agency budgets, funding organization administrators need to take into account the long-term consequences of fund reductions. Many human services are predicated on the idea of paying a small amount now for prevention or short-term care to avoid paying much more later for intensive treatment. Human service agency executives should be encouraged to provide specific information on the long-term consequences (financial and otherwise) of declining revenues. Perhaps the application form should be used to obtain such information.

One of the primary tasks funding organization administrators can do is to reward agencies that develop and execute a good plan for coping with limited resources. Rather than cut their allocation by the amount saved, they should be given additional resources or at least not have their allocations reduced when other agencies are being cut. This gives the agency an incentive to be even more productive and in a cost-effective way. With a policy of rewarding cost-effective agencies, taxpayers and those who donate funds are getting more for their dollar. What more could a funding organization ask?

There is much a funding organization can do to help agencies implement many of the suggestions made earlier in this chapter. The simultaneous link to numerous human services gives funding

organizations the opportunity to promote interagency cooperation. The funding organization can suggest arrangements for
joint purchasing, use of common services, or sharing personnel.
The funding organization can get the right people together and
smooth the bureaucratic tangles that often get in the way of
interagency cooperation.

Funding organization staff are in a good position to organize
half-day workshops on such topics as methods of costing services,
making office procedures more efficient, and writing grant
applications. Moreover, funding organization staff could institute
management assistance programs that would help agencies
implement suggestions made earlier in the chapter. Of course, it
would have to be done in a way that would avoid being interpreted
as direct involvement in the management of the agency. Perhaps
consultants (paid or volunteer) from other agencies could provide
the assistance.

Finally, funding organizations should themselves engage in
new revenue raising efforts so that they can do a better job of
funding the work of the agencies they help.

Chapter 2

ASSESSING PROGRAM EFFECTIVENESS AND DOCUMENTING NEED

INTRODUCTION

In times of reduced resources for human service programs, funders look for every possible way to justify cutback decisions. That a program is not operating effectively or that the need for a program is low or diminishing are grounds for cutting allocations. Therefore, it is in the agency's interest to be able to document effective performance and a need for the program. In addition to defending against cuts, information on effectiveness and need is just sound management. It allows agency administrators to detect problems when they first emerge and to take steps to deal with them before they get out of hand. Finally, low priority programs sometimes receive a larger increase (or less of a cut) than higher rated programs simply because they are well run and can show they are doing an effective job with the resources at hand, and that there is clear evidence the program is needed.

WHAT IS PROGRAM EFFECTIVENESS?

Effectiveness may be viewed as the quantity and quality of resources marshalled to serve those in need on the one hand and the number and quality of services delivered on the other. Both resources and services are indicators of effectiveness. Consider resources. It is to an agency's credit if the director can recruit and hold on to highly trained and experienced staff. Similarly, an agency that is able to acquire new dollars, equipment, or facilities is deemed effective. Attracting large numbers of volunteers is also a mark of effectiveness.

On the services side, serving a large number of clients,

19

providing each client with numerous services, and causing significant numbers of clients to achieve the desired outcome are all indicators of effectiveness. The relationship between resources and services is an indicator efficiency, a very crucial element when faced with resource cutbacks. The cost per unit of service or the number of services provided per staff member indicate how well the agency is doing with the resources available. Of course, if cost per client gets too low or each staff member is seeing too many clients, desired outcomes may decline. Effectiveness, then, is to become as efficient as possible without decreasing the desired outcomes.

MEASURES OF PROGRAM EFFECTIVENESS

Many human service professional associations have already established measures of effectiveness. These may be identified as standards of performance or criteria for accredidation. Professional associations tend to emphasize the resources that need to be allocated to achieve the desired outcome. For example, for a family counseling program, the accreditation body may suggest that to maximize outcomes, every counselor should have a masters degree in counseling, or that a counselor should have no more than twenty-five active cases. While these standards are worthy, they do neglect the productivity side of the effectiveness equation.

Such professional standards put the agency director in a dilemma. While the accreditation only stresses resources, local funding organizations are more concerned about providing services efficiently. The executive must try to balance these competing orientations. As many of the professional standards were derived at a time when funds were more available, the agency director may be able to compromise the resources and still maintain favorable levels of client outcomes. When client outcomes begin to decline (for details on monitoring client outcomes, see Chapter 3), then he/she knows no further compromises are possible.

Resources compromises may take the form of increasing staff competence through in-service training rather than through formal course work. Or, it may mean adding paraprofessionals and having the most qualified staff provide the necessary supervision.

We turn now to some ways to monitor effectiveness through a few simple record keeping procedures. We start by describing measures of resources after which assessments of services are suggested. Finally, we show that resource and service indicators can be combined into measures of efficiency.

Resources

1. The *total number of dollars* generated is an overall index of effectiveness, because it indicates the initiative of the agency staff. Of course, simply generating grants and awards can lead to ineffectiveness if the many projects spread staff too thin or detract from the agency's mission.

2. The *number of sources of funds* can also be a mark of effectiveness, as it indicates diverse sources of support that may be essential to remain viable in periods of cutback. Typically, not all sources are cut at the same time.

3. The *amount of self-generated funds* from user fees and fund raising projects (e.g., marathons, sales, or raffles) tends to be viewed favorably. Again, it indicates initiative and imagination.

4. The *proportion of staff with professional accreditation* indicates the extent to which professional staff have the qualifications to do an effective job.

5. The *proportion of staff with three to five years experience* shows that clients are likely to get high quality services. Low levels of experience may indicate turnover problems. Staff with high levels of experience may sometimes index deadwood, people who are not very productive and therefore are not attractive to competing employers.

6. The *number of volunteers* (in agencies that can use them) is also a resource that agencies can marshall to reduce workload of paid staff and increase effectiveness.

7. *Facilities*, and sometimes *equipment*, are important to providing quality service and therefore may be used as an indicator of effectiveness. Quality may be assessed in terms of age, clients per facility or piece of equipment, and

whether the facilities or equipment is "state of the art."
8. *Accreditation and awards* the agency receives is another indicator of effectiveness. The fact that this form of recognition comes from outside the agency gives the index additional weight.

These indices of resources can be used separately or together in documenting the effectiveness of an agency or program. Comparing current year resources with those of previous years results in an indication of improvement or trouble. Increased effectiveness can be used to argue for additional resources or to protect the ones the agency already has. A drop in effectiveness alerts agency executives to problems needing attention before they become difficult to solve. The information gleened by contrasting one's own agency on these resource measures with similar agencies in other cities can also be used to gain resources and troubleshoot problems.

Services Provided

1. The *number of clients* served is a basic indicator of productivity. Of course, clients sometimes increase because of a change in the law, a shift in the demographic composition of the community, or public attention to the problem (e.g., few people were concerned about spouse abuse a few years ago, although the incidence of the offense has changed little in recent decades). These intervening factors should be taken into account when using the number of clients indicator. For example, if one can show that the number of clients has actually increased faster than demographic changes, then the increase represents a real gain in effectiveness.
2. The *number of units of service* delivered is another mark of effectiveness. To be used successfully, a unit of service must have a clear, unequivocal definition, and the procedure for counting units and keeping records must be easy to use, part of everyday routine, and resistant to fudging.
3. The number of *services per client* is still another way of indexing productivity. Of course, there is the risk that if each client receives too many services, the quality of the service may go down. Regular checks of client outcomes will reveal whether or not quality is diminishing.

4. *Proportion of clients who experience the desired outcome* is an indicator of effectiveness that is sometimes hard to assess. Specific methods for monitoring outcomes are detailed in the next chapter. Because desired outcomes is a powerful mark of effectiveness, it should be used whenever possible.

5. *Proportion of staff (or full-time equivalents) providing direct service to clients* can be a mark of effectiveness. If the proportion gets too high, however, nobody is running the store and the agency can become inefficient and sloppy. If it is too low, the costs go up, and morale may decline because of supervision that does not allow employees enough autonomy. Administrators looking around for something to do often monitor employees more than they need to.

Like resources, current service performance can be compared with earlier years and comparable agencies. The results of comparison can be used to increase or maintain allocations and for the early detection of problems.

Resources and Services

1. *Cost per unit of service* is derived by dividing all of the program's expenses by the number of units of service provided in a year or some other period. Whether or not to include overhead depends on what other agencies in the community do or what the national professional association recommends. Use data that is going to make the strongest case with potential funders while staying in touch with the practice of other professionals. In times of limited resources, the cost per unit of service is an important indicator to monitor. And, if agency directors don't monitor it, funding organizations may take over the task and do an incomplete or poor analysis.

2. *Units of service per staff member* is derived by dividing the total number of units of service delivered by the number of full-time equivalent staff. This measure can be used to indicate whether staff are underutilized, efficient, or overworked. An overworked staff may cause declines in desired outcomes. Services per staff member can be used to answer critics who claim that costs are rising when, in

fact, the staff is just as efficient as it has ever been, and the cost increases are occurring in areas over which the agency has little control (e.g., wages, utilities, etc.).

3. *Cost per desired outcome* is calculated by dividing the total costs of the program by the number of clients who have achieved the desired outcome. Such figures can be compared to the costs to the community if clients are not served. Such data can often be used to make a powerful case to funders for maintaining or increasing resources.

CHANGES IN EFFECTIVENESS

Assessing effectiveness is an easy task having high payoffs. It is simple because the information needed to measure effectiveness is probably already being collected in some form. Expenditures are calculated routinely, especially at budget preparation time. Information on staff is available from personnel records, and data on clients and services is collected as a matter of course. In some cases, the information might not be collected in the form needed to assess effectiveness, but it can be with modest effort. Thus, with the possible exception of client outcomes, monitoring effectiveness is a matter of pulling together information that is already in hand.

As one monitors change in the effectiveness indicators from year to year, the question comes up — what constitutes a significant change? Does a drop of a few cents in the cost per unit of service represent an increase in efficiency? It depends on three things: the number of services, the magnitude of the expense in providing a service, and the period of time. If the number of services provided each year is small, say 4,000, a drop of 10¢ amounts to $400. This is not much money if the overall budget is $100,000, but it is an amount to notice if the total budget is $3,500. If the drop occurs one year and goes up the next, the change is less remarkable than if it occurs for three or four years in a row. By taking into account number of services, magnitude of expense, and the period of time, the agency director can decide whether or not he/she should use the information or ignore it.

To use information on effectiveness as part of a report to the board, fund application, or client recruitment drive is straight forward. To use it for trouble shooting or a management decision is more complex. For example, an effectiveness index may only be an indirect indicator of a problem. To begin to trace the difficulty, a line item analysis of income and expenses may reveal what changes are occurring that account for the alteration in effectiveness. If clients are involved in the shift, check the census for changes in the composition of the population in the community from which the clients come. A drop in the size of the youth cohort, a rise in the elderly population, or a decline in people employed in primary industry (those requiring unskilled labor) can significantly alter the need for services. Scan professional association newsletters for national trends that might account for the changes that are occuring. Internal strife should be examined as a source for a drop in effectiveness. A new employee or two, or a change in office procedure can bring about dramatic changes in effectiveness. These and other possibilities need to be examined to identify the source of the change in effectiveness.

In addition to trouble shooting and strengthening funding applications, effectiveness measures can be used to chart the impact of new approaches or procedures. If one attempts to improve the staff by offering more attractive salaries, the qualifications of the staff can be assessed after a year or two of operation under the new policy to see if the average years of formal training or years of experience have increased or not. The effectiveness of a new program for recruiting volunteers can be assessed by comparing the number of volunteers or clients per volunteer before and after the program began. If a new method of providing service is implemented, the proportion of clients who have achieved the desired outcomes can be compared before and after the program was changed. A systematic effort to cut expenses can be monitored by reviewing the cost per unit of service before and after the change was implemented.

In all attempts to assess the effect of change, effectiveness should be monitored long after the change was implemented. The reason for this is that a change usually results in improved performance because staff are conscious of being observed and are influenced by the excitement of making an alteration in the routine. Termed the Hawthorn effect (after the man who first described the phenomena), a long trial period is necessary to make sure the effect of the innovation is not temporary.

COMPARISONS OF THE PROGRAM WITH THOSE
IN OTHER AGENCIES AND WITH
NATIONAL STANDARDS

While monitoring changes in one's own agency is useful and important, comparison with practices elsewhere is just as vital. It is easy to become so involved in managing the affairs of the organization that one forgets there are other ways to accomplish the same objectives and perhaps more efficient ones. Regular comparison can bring fresh ideas to the operation that may enhance effectiveness.

Some national professional associations collect effectiveness information and pass it along to member agencies. Comparison with national figures can be helpful. But, because national figures are based on the performance of agencies in a wide variety of social and economic settings, they may not represent a valid comparison for some agencies.

Central to valid comparisons is the selection of agencies that operate in similar settings such that their clientele, population in need, and sources of funding are similar. If the agency is located in a large metropolitan area, one may be able to locate organizations for comparison in other areas of the city. However, demographic variation is great in most metropolitan areas; therefore, a suitable comparison may not be found.

Selecting agencies in similar cities or areas involves a few minutes in the library to look up the characteristics of candidates for comparison. If selecting agencies from the same community, check the 1980 census and see if the tracts in which similar agencies are located are comparable to your own with respect to the age, marital status, race, and income of the residents. The librarian can help you find the references containing Census tract information. When selecting other communities, a ready guide is the *Municipal Year Book* and the most recent *City County Data Book*. Go through the yearbook and identify communities that are no more than 25 percent larger or smaller than your own. The *Yearbook* also has information on population change, an important factor to take into account.

If your community is growing at a moderate rate, eliminate cities that are declining in population or growing much more rapidly than your own. Population change has a remarkable

CITIES SIMILAR TO LINCOLN ON SELECTED CHARACTERISTICS PERTINENT TO THE PROVISION OF HUMAN SERVICES*

City	Population in 1000s	Change in Population from 1970-80	Percent of Work Force Manufacturing	Percent Below Federal Poverty Guidelines	Per Capita Local Current Expenditures for Education, Highways, Public Welfare and Health	Percent Black	Percent Hispanic
Lincoln, NE	172	13	12	6	365	2	2
Anchorage, AK	173	37	3	5	894	5	3
Amarillo, TX	149	17	11	9	628	6	9
Colorado Springs, CO	215	53	11	9	379	6	8
Des Moines, IA	191	(5)	19	6	456	7	2
Knoxville, TN	183	5	27	15	287	14	1
Lexington, KY	204	17	19	11	246	13	1
Madison, WI	171	(1)	13	16	351	3	1
Salt Lake City, UT	163	(7)	14	7	298	2	8
Springfield, IL	133	11	14	7	277	2	1
Spokane, WA	171	0	12	9	324	2	1
Tacoma, WA	159	3	19	8	358	9	2

( ) Decline in population

* Data on population, population change, and race from 1982 Municipal Year Book. Remainder of information from 1977 City County Data Book.

effect on the economy of a community and is, therfore, a key factor to consider. Percent of the work force employed in manufacturing is an indicator of the economic base and the skill level of the work force. Percent below federal poverty guidelines is a factor that is a rough measure of the size of the client population for a good many human services. The per capita local expenditures for education, highways, public welfare, and health suggests the extent of the community's commitment to providing human services. Percent black and Hispanic indicate the social composition of the community. The proportion of the young and the elderly are other features that may be important in selecting comparable cities. These last items of information are found in the *City County Data Book*. Cities that vary considerably from your own on any of the variables important to your operation should be eliminated from consideration as candidates for comparison. We suggest putting together a table (such as the one on page 27) of all cities that have a similar population and rate of growth or decline. List all of the information on those cities. Then go through and cross off those that are dissimilar on any feature that might make the agency in that community very different from your own.

Once a list of comparable communities has been compiled, get the names of agency directors from the membership lists of your national professional association. Write to them requesting effectiveness information that would be easy for them to provide. Offer, in return, a compilation of the data you collect. The offer to share information is a strong incentive to cooperate. A letter to selected agency directors might say the following.

Dear————:
In these times of scarce dollars for human services, we are called upon to make our case for funds stronger each year. Increasingly, we are asked to provide comparative information showing that our programs are not out of line with respect to the efficiency and the effectiveness with which we deliver our services. It is in this connection that I am writing to you.

As you know, good comparative information is hard to find. Therefore we have taken it upon ourselves to collect some basic data on (types of programs) program in cities that are demographically and socially similar to (name of your city). A copy of the list of cities to which I am sending this request, along with the demographics, is enclosed for your information. As you well know, it would be silly to compare our operation with those in much larger or much smaller cities, or with cities that face quite different problems than we do.

I enclose a brief questionnaire in which I request information on the number of staff, dollars spent, and units of service delivered during a recent twelve month period for your (type of program) program. I know your schedule is already busy, but I would very much appreciate it if you could return the completed questionnaire to me no later than (date 10 days from date sent) so that I can include summary information in my current budget request. A stamped, self-addressed envelope has been enclosed for your convenience. In return, I will send you photostats of all the responses I receive, plus information on my own program, so that you can make use of the information as well.

There is the matter of confidentiality. While I don't mind if you identify the information on my program as coming from (name of city), other executives may. If anyone of the respondents does object, I will remove identifying information from all of the forms except yours before sending them to you. I will send a list of the cities that did respond so you will know to what universe the data is applicable.

I hope you will join me in this effort. The additional information can help each of us in these austere times. If you have any questions

about this form or the procedures, give me a call at
(your phone).

Cordially,

The questionnaire you enclose should be short and simple. If possible, fit it on a single page. If you are collecting information on several programs, prepare a separate form for each and indicate you are requesting information on more than one program in the letter. A sample form appears on the page 32. Some of the sample questions may not be relevant, and others may need to be added. You may want to ask for their definitions of successful outcomes if they are likely to be different from your own.

Once compiled, it is important to present information on several cities. Comparisons with one other community would not be very convincing. People will suspect that the most favorable case was selected for comparison. On the other hand, you may have trouble finding half a dozen agencies that bear a strong resemblance to your own. When presenting the information, unless there is information on at least ten agencies, it is probably not worthwhile to calculate averages or make frequency distributions. A simple listing in order of effectiveness may be the most suitable way to present the information.

The information from other organizations may contain some surprises. There may be some organizations that are extraordinarily more effective or ineffective. It is worth while trying to identify the reasons for the variability. Executives of very effective programs may be willing to share information (and may even be flattered that you ask) about their operation that may help in making your organization more effective. On the other hand, you may find the differences are due to variation in the way units of service are defined or in allocating expenses and therefore gain little that is new.

DOCUMENTING NEED FOR PROGRAMS

To plan effectively, executives need to know the number of individuals in their service area that are in need of the agency's services. It is important to know the absolute number so that an estimate can be made of the size of the populations that is not being reached. Also, information on whether the population in need is increasing or decreasing is vital. The number of persons needing services can be used as a basis for arriving at a budget and as a justification for program expansion. Or, in the case of a declining population in need, such figures can be used to explain a shift in emphasis to serve other unmet needs. Basic figures on need can be put to good use in promotional materials, governing board orientations, and in every application for funds.

Documenting need seldom is easy. Unless one has access to community survey data (of a type described in Chapter 5), often only indirect estimates are possible. Professional associations sometimes sponsor studies that document the size of the population in need nationally. On the basis of such studies, the national association may ascertain that a certain percent of the population is in need of the service. Local agencies may apply that figure to local census information on population size and come up with a defensible figure. For example, it may be estimated that 13 percent of the households in the country with persons 65 and over are in need of in-home services, such as cleaning, maintenance, or lawn care, in order for the occupants to remain independent. By consulting census publications at the local library, the agency executive learns that there are 20,000 households with elderly residents in his/her community or service area. By multiplying the 20,000 households by 13 percent, he/she learns that there may be 2,600 households in need of the services provided. By subtracting from that figure the number of households being serviced by agencies providing such services, one can estimate the number with unmet needs.

Census data provides precise estimates of the number of people (and households containing people) in various age, income, racial, employment, and marital and parental categories by census tract, city, county, and metropolitan area. Thus, if your agency deals primarily with youth between the ages of fourteen and twenty-four, the precise number in your service area can be obtained by consulting census publications at the local library. Similarly, the number of young mothers, blacks, or low income persons can be obtained from census documents.

COMPARATIVE INFORMATION STUDY OF
_____ PROGRAMS

To make sure we are not comparing apples and oranges, I provide the following brief description of our program. (In 2 or 3 sentences, indicate the nature of target population and types of services provided program clients.)

If your program varies from this description significantly, please indicate specific ways in which it is different.

_____

_____

_____

Selecting a recent twelve-month period for which you have figures (preferably a budget year), provide the following information. If you don't have exact information, any information given will be better than no information at all.

A. Total dollar amount that covers direct costs of this program
   $_____

B. Number full-time equivalent staff assigned to program:
   Administrative   _____
   Professional   _____
   Support   _____

C. What percent of your professional staff have (appropriate degree, certification or other credentials) _____ %.

D. Volunteers
   Number of people   _____
   Full-time equivalent   _____

E. Number of units of service provided. We use those listed below. Provide information in comparable units, if possible. If not possible, or you use additional ones, define them and indicate number provided in twelve-month period.

   1. (list your unit of service)   _____
   2. (list your unit of service)   _____
   _____   _____
   _____   _____

F. What percent of your clients complete the program _____?
   (or)
   What percent of your clients enjoy successful outcomes _____?

Combining national figures with census data may not always yield an accurate estimate. In the case of the example given above, if the local community was economically depressed, the need might be higher. Or, if it was especially affluent, the number might be lower. National studies sometimes include an analysis of factors likely to influence the number in need. There may be enough detail in their reports to adjust your own estimates of those in need. By examining the research reports themselves, one can get an idea of any problems there might be in applying national figures to the local scene.

Some national studies contain information on the costs of letting problems go unattended. Usually the figure is much higher than the cost of serving clients. Agency executives should draw on such estimates in presenting their case.

RECOMMENDATIONS FOR FUNDING ORGANIZATION ADMINISTRATORS

Funders should insist that agencies provide hard information on effectiveness and need. It is not unreasonable to refuse to review applications where that information is omitted or of very low quality.

Once provided, however, it is important that it be used. Effectiveness should not be taken as an article of faith, and allocations based only on error free balance sheets, or testimonials from satisfied clients. Rather, effectiveness and need data should be tied directly to funding decisions. A mechanism should be in place to systematically take effectiveness and need information into account in reaching allocations decisions. Some of these mechanisms are spelled out in detail in Chapter 4.

On the other hand, it is important not to over interpret short-term trends (e.g., a one-year decline or increase). All phenomena go through fluctuations, many of which are relatively meaningless. Also, one should not base substantive decisions on indirect estimates. The error rate for such estimates is often high. Rather, the agency should be encouraged to obtain better data.

Chapter 3

MONITORING CLIENT OUTCOMES

Most human service agencies have developed techniques for monitoring client progress while they are in the program. Information about the client's condition is obtained when they begin and again when they terminate, whether or not they completed the program. What is lacking in many human service areas is an inexpensive and effective method for learning what happens to clients after leaving the program. While follow-up study in programs where clients are anonymous (e.g., crisis line), never leave (e.g., programs for the terminally ill), or are transients is not possible, in most programs there is opportunity to contact clients once they are no longer receiving help from agency staff.

Continuous monitoring of client outcomes is especially important in hard times. Funding organizations are more likely to question the benefits of programs and are less likely to take for granted that such programs are needed. Preventive programs, such as those offered by youth development agencies (Y, Scouts, community centers), often come out low in priority studies. In part, this is because the preventive claim is often unsubstantiated by outcome studies. Finally, funding organization staff and volunteers often have a very incomplete understanding of outcomes. They often don't recognize, for example, that a drug treatment program not only affects the client, but influences the client's relations with family members, friends, and coworkers and the client's ability to go to school or hold down a job. Funding organizations may not recognize that a youth who plays basketball at the community center after school is not only keeping out of trouble, but is developing a skill that pays off in school, increases self-confidence, leads to new friends, relieves parental anxieties about his/her whereabouts or activities, provides contact with good role models, and so on. All of these are outcomes that may occur after the individual leaves the program.

By systematically collecting outcome information on a continuous basis, the agency gains information that can be used to demonstrate the effectiveness of its programs to funding organizations, critics, and potential clients. In addition, outcome information can be used to evaluate the effectiveness of various aspects of the program. The outcomes of clients who had contact with one staff member can be compared with those whose contact was with another. Clients receiving services by a new method can be compared with those experiencing a traditional approach to determine which track is more effective. Outcomes of clients who have been in the program for different lengths of time can be compared to determine the optimum time needed to achieve a particular outcome. Once optimum time is determined, special efforts can be made to keep clients for the needed period and clients who have been in for the necessary period may be encouraged to obtain a less costly form of help. Follow-up of people who had only cursory contact with the program can be used as a nontreatment group and compared with those who actually complete the program to determine whether they are worse off than those who continued with the agency.

Moreover, follow-up may become part of the treatment plan and benefit the client. Clients who have left the program and are experiencing difficulties may need personal contact to nudge them back into treatment. Or, clients may simply need reassurance that help is available if it is needed.

Follow-up study can be costly and time-consuming so that it does not justify the effort. But it need not be. Step-by-step procedures for implementing a simple, inexpensive tested and effective follow-up study are presented below. Detailed instructions and sample forms for tracking clients, interviewing them by telephone, assembling and presenting information are shown. The study procedure is especially designed for small and moderately-sized programs staffed with people having little or no evaluation experience. Nearly all of the work can be carried out by support staff in a few hours per month.

OVERVIEW OF THE FOLLOW-UP PROCEDURE

The follow-up study procedure described here is based on one developed and tested in a drug and alcohol treatment program. To give substance to the examples the drug and alcohol designations are retained. However, the example is easily translated into other types of programs, as many of the goals are the same—to help clients be productive and healthy citizens. As an aid in keeping track of the various parts of the follow-up study, the name of the separate follow-up study forms, instructions, and records that follow are set in italic type.

Follow-up study begins when the client leaves the program. At that time, a calendar entry is made three months hence to remind the individual responsible for interviewing clients to begin to try to reach the client. The name, address, and phone number of the client are transferred from the admission or dismissal form to the *Tracking Record,* a form designed to record progress in reaching the client. Names, addresses, and phone numbers of people most likely to know the whereabouts of the client are also recorded on the *Tracking Record.* Summary information on the client and his progress in the program is transferred to the first two pages on the *Interview Schedule* (questionnaire).

On the appointed day, the interviewer begins to try to reach the client using the *Tracking Instructions* as a guideline. Once located, the client is interviewed and his/her responses recorded on the *Interview Schedule.* Information contained in the *Interviewing Instructions* should guide the interview.

After the interview is completed, the *Interview Schedule* should be checked for accuracy and completion and the *Tracking Record* destroyed so that interview responses cannot be linked to the client. The interview data can then be entered directly into a computer for analysis, or, if the caseload is small (a few hundred cases), the interview data can be transferred to a *Tabulation Form.* *Summaries* can then be generated at will for such things as planning, evaluation, board meetings, annual reports, publicity, and fund applications.

SETTING UP THE STUDY

The key to setting up a follow-up study that works and becomes a regular part of the agency's operation is keeping it simple.

There is a tendency for administrators beginning such projects to gather too much information, because they can see so many ways to use the data. Collect no more information than is found on the sample interview. Do not attempt analysis any more complex than that which is proposed. More complex studies are almost certain to fail, as they make too many demands on limited staff and resources and are difficult to incorporate into the routine of the agency's operation. Only after the follow-up study has become second nature (after one or two years of operation) should more complex elements of information and analysis be introduced.

Assign someone the primary responsibility for tracking, interviewing, and tabulating the information. A receptionist, secretary, or other staff support can do the work in a few hours each month. As a guide to planning the workload, the study described here was for an agency that had a caseload of 50 residential clients and 130 outpatients. It usually takes three trys to reach the client (it may take fewer attempts if the client population is less transient), and the interview itself averages 15 minutes. It usually takes no more than one hour per month to tabulate the interview data and produce a report similar to the one at the end of this chapter.

Before beginning, a decision needs to be made about which clients to follow up and which to omit. If you do not need information on people who elected not to take part in the program (to prove that participation has more impact than nonparticipation), then it makes sense to exclude those who have only completed the application form, come to an orientation session, or attended one or two meetings. In short, exclude individuals upon whom there has been no opportunity to have an impact. For the drug treatment program example used here, clients were excluded from follow-up study if they had less than five counseling sessions or five days in residence, because the agency is organized around a long-term treatment philosophy. Agency administrators will have to decide for themselves the criteria to use for the exclusion of clients from follow-up study participation. The criteria must be specific and simple so that staff responsible for follow-up can easily and quickly decide whether the individual is to be contacted or not.

A second decision that needs to be reached before beginning is the number of clients that need to be contacted to make follow-up a meaningful study. In each year's data there should be enough cases to make the analysis of the interview information reliable. In the drug/alcohol treatment program example used here, all clients were included because of the small case load. As a rule of thumb, there should be at least 100 cases in a subgroup (for example a mode of treatment) before using the data as a basis for major policy decisions. One can have more confidence in outcome information based on 200 cases. On the other hand, it is not worthwhile collecting information on more than 200 cases, as each additional follow-up client adds little that is new. Major trends will not be altered by the addition of another 100 cases. In fact, it is wasteful to collect more information than suggested above. Thus, for agencies that handle a large number of clients, a means must be devised to randomly exclude clients from follow-up study so that one ends up with just the right number of completed interviews each year. Random selection is important so that bias does not creep into the selection of clients for follow-up. We suggest using the year of the client's birth or the case number as a basis for selection. If the number of clients eligible to be interviewed is 400 and you want to try to contact 200 (which may result in about 130 completed interviews after refusals are taken into account), take those with an odd number year of birth (45, 53, 57, 51). If only two clients out of ten are needed, select those whose year of birth ends in, say, 5 and 7, or 2 and 4. If you need four clients out of 10, include those whose year of birth ends in 2, 4, 6, and 8, or some other four digits. These techniques insure unbiased selection.

A third decision that needs to be reached before beginning concerns the length of time you want to elapse before trying to contact the client. In the example, people with drug and alcohol problems tend to be a transient population. For this reason, three months was selected. Two thirds of the clients are interviewed with this amount of elapsed time. If one wanted to assess longer term effects in a transient population, a second follow-up interview could be conducted some six months after the first interview. That way you would have the early follow-up data and not run the risk of losing the opportunity to obtain information altogether. The length of time between terminating the program and follow-up can be longer for less transient populations. Six months would be appropriate for more stable populations. A suitable follow-up period is best decided by professional staff who are familiar with the client's style of life and the length of time needed for certain treatment outcomes to be realized.

TRACKING CLIENTS

Most human service agencies do not ask for the names of people who would know where the client is living after leaving the program as part of the admission or termination procedure. Thus, there will have to be some modification of application forms (or termination forms, if used) to obtain the information needed to track clients. While this information is only needed 15 percent of the time, being able to interview hard-to-reach clients adds much to the validity of follow-up study.

Therefore, in the course of admitting a client, the following information should be obtained: (1) the client's name, address, and phone number (if female and married, the husband's first name) and (2) the names, addresses, and phone numbers of three relatives or friends who would know where the client is living if he/she moved. A blood relative is a preferred source, but neighbors and employers are not good sources. The client might be told the following:

> As part of our effort to improve the services we provide, we interview clients after they have left our program to get their ideas on how the program should be changed. Sometimes people move even though they are not really planning to right now. Would you please give me the name and address of someone who would know where you lived if you happened to move in the next year or so—for example, a relative? I want you to understand that this person's name will not be used in any way except to help us locate you if you have moved. This person will not be interviewed nor will they be told about your contact with (name of program).

Staff should update the admission form whenever they become aware that the client has changed his/her phone number.

The instructions for tracking clients are presented on the

following pages. These are presented as if the reader is the person assigned to do the tracking. Following that is the *Tracking Record* itself. This is the form for recording progress in reaching the client. Be sure to go over each step of the instructions for tracking clients with the person who will be doing the tracking to be sure he/she understands each step. After they have a chance to use it a dozen times, review recent cases to see if there are any ways tracking procedures can be improved. Also, check to be sure every step was taken to try and reach those that could not be contacted.

Procedures for Tracking Former Clients

1. When a client leaves the program, an entry should be made in the calendar three months hence to remind the individual responsible for interviewing clients to begin to try to reach the client.

2. Transfer identifying and reference information (people who will know where the client is living) from the admission form to the first part of the *Tracking Record*.

3. Complete items 1 through 14 on the interview schedule using information from the termination and admission forms. (This is done so that all information needed to do follow-up study is on one form.)

4. On the appointed day, call the number listed on the *Tracking Record* and ask for the client. If the client answers, proceed with the interview. Otherwise, complete appropriate steps below. Record information on steps taken in the client's tracking record sheet.

    a. If the person answering the phone is not the client, ask for the client and proceed with the interview.

    b. If the client is not at home, obtain some estimate of when they will be home and call back at that time. If the client is not at home when you call back, continue to call back at least three different times when the client is likely to be at home.

    c. If the person answering the phone says the client does not live at that number, see if they know how the client can be reached or the name of someone who would know where the client could be reached. If so, use the information provided.

d. If the person answering the phone does not know of the client's whereabouts, check directory assistance in same city.

e. If directory assistance is of no help, call personal references that the client named at the time of admission and proceed with information they provide. Sometimes the personal references need to be tracked.

f. If there is no answer to the number the client provided for himself/herself or the personal reference, make at least three calls back on different days and different times, including weekends and evenings.

g. If the phone number is no longer in service, is continuously busy, or doesn't ring at all, proceed to subsequent steps in the tracking process.

h. If the client gave no phone number at the time of admission, check directory assistance in his or her city to see if one is listed under the client's name and address.

i. If all efforts to reach the client by phone fail, send a letter first class with a "return address requested" stamp. If the client has moved and left forwarding information, you will receive the new address from the post office. After indicating the purpose of the letter, ask the client to return a post card with current phone number or to call the interviewer collect.

j. If one of the personal references or a person other than the client asks about your identity and affiliation, simply say, "My name is _____ and Mr./Ms. (name of client is expecting me to call at this time."

k. Do not leave a phone message for the client to call you back.

l. Please keep a complete record of your attempts to contact the client on the client's tracking record. This will help you keep straight when you are in the process of tracking the client or will allow another interviewer to pick up where you left off. When you finish tracking (obtained the interview or exhausted all possibilities), destroy the tracking record. Be sure information from admission and termination forms have been transferred before destroying.

TRACKING RECORD

Information From Admission Form

Client's Full Name _____ Phone ( )_____
First   Middle   Last

Husband's First Name if Married Female _____

Last Known Address: Street _____ Apt. #_____

City _____

State _____ Zip Code_____

Personal References

1. Name: _____ _____ _____
Husband's First Name   Initial

Street: _____ Apt. _____

City _____ State _____ Zip Code _____ Phone ( )_____

2. Name: _____ _____ _____
Husband's First Name   Initial

Street: _____ Apt. _____

City _____ State _____ Zip Code _____ Phone ( )_____

3. Name: _____ _____ _____
Husband's First Name   Initial

Street: _____ Apt. _____

City _____ State _____ Zip Code _____ Phone ( )_____

Address and Telephone Record

As you track respondent to current address and telephone number, record all intervening addresses and telephone numbers on this record. Begin with the earliest known new location and continue until you reach the current address and telephone. Indicate source of information briefly on this chart and detail both successful and unsuccessful tracking efforts.

1. _____ _____ _____ _____ _____
   Street   City   Zip   Phone   Source

2. _____ _____ _____ _____ _____
   Street   City   Zip   Phone   Source

3. _____ _____ _____ _____ _____
   Street   City   Zip   Phone   Source

NAME CHANGED TO _____

Tracking Steps

Interviewer's Initials: _____   TRACKING STEP #1

Date: _____

Time: _____

_____

Interviewer's Initials: _____   TRACKING STEP #2

Date: _____

Time: _____

_____

Interviewer's Initials: _____   TRACKING STEP #3

Date: _____

Time: _____

_____

Interviewer's Initials: _____   TRACKING STEP #4

Date: _____

Time: _____

STAPLE ANOTHER SHEET TO THIS IF TRACKING REQUIRES ADDITIONAL STEPS. REMOVE FROM INTERVIEW SCHEDULE AND DESTROY THIS FORM WHEN TRACKING IS COMPLETED.

INTERVIEWING FORMER CLIENTS

"Why interview?" "Questionnaires are much less expensive." The answer to these much raised questions is that interviews glean more information and are effective in eliciting responses from hard to reach individuals. Many human service clients have limited reading and writing skills. For them, reading questions and writing answers is a task they are not used to and is considered to be hard work. Individuals not used to reading and writing answer incompletely or put off completing the questionnaire all together. The personal interview is simple, direct, and more effective in obtaining answers to all of the questions. The phone interview is now replacing door-to-door interviews because it is less expensive. Studies have shown that it is as effective as household interviews in getting hard-to-reach populations. A very high proportion of the population (90% to 95%) have telephones. In short, phone interviewing is an effective and inexpensive method of gathering information from former clients.

Experience indicates that while a few clients resent being contacted, the majority appreciate the concern reflected by the interview. Even most of those who do not successfully complete the program are not put off by the interview.

In training the person who is going to do the interviewing, go over the following instructions verbally after they have had a chance to read them and become familiar with the interview schedule. Have the interviewer go through a practice interview with another employee playing the role of the client. Discuss the interview afterwards, suggesting different ways to solve problems.

Then have the individual do three telephone interviews with former clients, with the supervisor listening. The supervisor need not be on another phone, just nearby. Again, the interviews should be discussed. It is also a good idea to check over the first ten completed schedules to make sure all of the items have been completed. Review any omissions with the interviewer.

The interviewing instructions used to train staff persons are on the following pages. These are presented as if the reader is the person assigned to do the interviewing.

Interviewing Instructions

1. When you contact the client, use something similar to the following introduction:

> I am _____, an interviewer from (Name of Agency). According to our records, you completed our program about three months ago. We are calling to get your ideas on aspects of the program that could be improved and on factors that you thought were strong points. The information you provide will be kept confidential. The people you had (as counselors, representing you, helping you, or some other appropriate designation) will never be able to connect you with anything you might say. The information you provide will be combined with that provided by other people and presented in summary form only.

DO NOT ASK THE CLIENT IF YOU MAY INTERVIEW HIM/HER. MERELY BEGIN BY ASKING QUESTION 20 ON THE INTERVIEW SCHEDULE.

2. Ask all of the questions in the order and wording indicated.

3. After the interview, check to make sure all questions have been asked. If not, call back.

4. Complete postinterview rating. This will help in evaluating quality of the information you received.

5. If the client refuses to answer a question, go on (without comment) to the next question.

6. Do not act surprised, pleased, or disappointed by *any* information the client gives you. The most reliable information is obtained when the interviewer is neutral.

7. Do *not*, under any circumstances, relay information on an individual client to any staff member or outsider. Confidentiality is crucial to the success of the evaluation. Not only does it break a promise given to a client, but it sometimes leaks back to the client, and his/her confidence in the agency is weakened.

8. If the client is suspicious or raises questions about confidentiality, reassure him/her by saying something like the following:

> I understand your reluctance. I can assure you that the information you provide is not associated with your name in any way. As soon as I hang up the phone, the page with your name and phone number is removed and destroyed. There is no way that staff at (*name of agency*) or anyone else will know what you said.

9. If the client wonders whether you are legitimate or not, say,

> If you would like to verify that this is a proper study, I can give you a number you can call collect so that you can reassure yourself.

IF THEY ELECT TO DO IT, GIVE THEM THE NUMBER OF THE AGENCY DIRECTOR OR OTHER QUALIFIED PERSON DESIGNATED TO HANDLE SUCH CALLS AND SAY, "I will call you back after you finish."

10. If the answer categories don't fit what the respondent says, record the client's words in the margin.

11. Record answers to precoded questions by circling the number next to the appropriate category.

12. For open-ended questions (where there are no categories), record the exact wording the client used, leaving out redundant or irrelevant material.

13. If you have any questions or problems, ask (name of person responsible for study).

THE INTERVIEW SCHEDULE

The interview schedule itself is the cornerstone of follow-up study. The quality of follow-up rests or falls on the way the questions are asked, the ordering of the questions, and the layout of the schedule. In the following paragraphs, the interview schedule will be described and the reasons for particular features given. As you read each paragraph, refer to the appropriate section of the interview schedule.

The letters **ID** that appear at the top of the first page refer to an identification number that is assigned after the interview is completed. The number is helpful in keeping track of the follow-up study and correcting errors.

Tracking information at the top of the schedule provides data on the length of time after leaving the program that the respondent was interviewed. The time between contact with the agency and the interview may have some bearing on the type or extent of impact the agency has had. Also, the dates allow one to link outcomes to changes in the program. If the program undergoes a major change in 1985, a comparison of client outcomes before and after that date can indicate the impact of the alterations on the client.

Whether or not the *interview is obtained* is optional information that some agencies may find useful and others not. It is useful when one wishes to keep information on those that cannot be reached in the follow-up study. People that cannot be reached may be compared with those that are contacted to see if unreachables are more likely to terminate before completing the program. By excluding them, success rates would be overestimated. If the incompletes are not different from those that are interviewed, one can have more confidence that the follow-up data applies to all clients, regardless of whether they can be reached for an interview.

Admission and termination information (items 1 thru 19) on the first two pages of the schedule is basic to follow-up study analysis. It is information on the condition of the clients at the time they enter the program that must be compared with the follow-up information to see what outcomes have been achieved. Information on the clients when they leave the program, when compared to follow-up interview data, indicate whether the gains that have been made are retained after leaving the program. In the example drug treatment program, the goals are to have clients obtain employment or continue their education, reduce drug use, enhance interpersonal relations, and reduce depression and anxiety. Items 1 thru 17 are the admission and termination information that pertains to these matters. The items in this part of the interview schedule should be in the same order as they appear on the admission and termination records, to simplify the transfer of information. In many cases, agencies that embark on follow-up study may find that they do not obtain information pertinent to outcomes at the time of admission, at least in a form that is comparable to follow-up questions that would be asked of clients over the telephone. Questions may have to be added to the admission interview or application form that are the same as those asked during the follow-up interview. For comparisons to be valid, the exact wording must be used.

The background information (age, sex, marital status, prior treatment) is helpful in learning whether some individuals benefit from the program more than others. The program information (weeks in treatment, type of treatment, identification of counselor, type of termination) is useful in identifying aspects of the program that enjoy more success than others.

Finally, to keep the follow-up information all together for each client, the first two pages of the interview schedule are kept with the tracking record until the client is reached or classified as unreachable. In this way, all the information is in one place, and files are not cluttered up with empty interviews. The remainder of the interview schedule is added once the interview is completed. After checking to make sure all of the items have been answered, the *Tracking Record* is removed and destroyed.

Client evaluation of the program (questions 20 thru 24) items are optional. They can be of help in (1) identifying staff that need assistance, (2) assessing client satisfaction, and (3) spotting aspects of the program that need some work and others that are doing well. These questions can be used for internal evaluation and planning, as well as for reporting program effectiveness to board members and other interested parties. These questions serve another function as well. They get the clients warmed up for questions about themselves. They are nonthreatening questions that give the client a chance to develop trust in the interviewer.

Outcome questions (items 25 thru 35) are simple and direct. There are some aspects of human service goals that are more complex than these questions indicate. The fact that some individuals responding to the questions have considerable ability to make distinctions, and to others, very little means that some of the subtleties of outcome possibilities must be sacrificed to obtain comparable information on as many clients as possible.

The open-ended wrap-up question (item 36) is optional. It occurs at the end of the interview, after the client has been thinking about the program for several minutes. Thus, it has the potential for providing new information. Sometimes it yields information that earlier questions do not tap. Most of the time it does not. Agencies might leave it in for 100 interviews and, if the yield is small, drop it.

The postinterview ratings (items 37 thru 41) are useful in

assessing the quality of the information obtained. If it appears that the information from a particular client is unreliable, you may wish to omit that respondent from some aspects of the analysis. They should be retained, however, so that responses can be compared with admission and termination information to see whether a particular type of client is unresponsive to follow-up study.

Notice that the interview schedule is short. Every item that is added is expensive both in time to conduct the interview and in the resources needed to tabulate and process the information. The sample interview schedule is at the upper limit of time to administer for modest-sized human service agencies.

Follow-up Interview Schedule

I.D. __ __ __ __

	Month	Day	Year
DATE TRACKING STARTED:	__ __ /	__ __ /	__ __
DATE TRACKING COMPLETED:	__ __ /	__ __ /	__ __

INTERVIEW:

Obtained 1

Not obtained 2

Information for items 1 thru 19 should be transferred from the admission and termination forms at the time the tracking record is filled out and date set to begin tracking.

1. Age—

YEARS ..... __ __

2. Sex—

Male 1

Female .. 2

3. Prior Treatment—

None 1

Name of agency doing follow-up

study 2

Other program 3

4. Legal Status Before Treatment—

No history of trouble with

law 1

In trouble with law 2

5. Getting along with friends recently—

> Very well 1
> Pretty well 2
> Not too well ... 3
> Don't have
>   friends 4
> Don't know 8
> Refused 9

6. Getting along with parents—

> Very well 1
> Pretty well 2
> Not too well 3
> Don't have parents . 4
> Don't know 8
> Refused 9

7. Get along with opposite sex—

> Very well 1
> Pretty well 2
> Not too well 3
> Don't have contact . 4
> Don't know 8
> Refused 9

8. Angry—

> Most of the time .. 1
> Some of the time . 2
> Once in a while .. 3
> Never 4
> Don't know 8
> Refused 9

9. Depressed—

                              Most of the time .. 1
                              Some of the time . 2
                              Once in a while .. 3
                              Never 4
                              Don't know 8
                              Refused 9

10. Education at conclusion of treatment—

                    Less than high school grad ... 1
                    GED or high school diploma . 2
                    Post high school training 3

11. Employment at conclusion of treatment—

                              Unemployed .. 1
                              Part-time 2
                              Full-time 3

12. Marital status at conclusion of treatment—

                         Never married 1
                         Married 2
                         Divorced/Separated .. 3
                         Widowed 4

13. Education obtained during treatment—

                    Did not go to school 1
                    Went to school—did not
                      complete program 2
                    Went to school—did complete
                      program 3

14. Employment during treatment—

> Did not work 1
> Worked 2
> Obtained job—retained 3
> Obtained job—did not retain . 4

15. Counselor—

    1. _____
    2. _____
    3. _____

16. Weeks in treatment—

> WEEKS ..... _ _

17. Type of treatment—

> Residential 1
> Outpatient 2
> Residential and
>   Outpatient 3

18. Termination—

> Completed 01
> Voluntary discharge with
>   staff approval 02
> Voluntary discharge without
>   staff approval 03
> Staff dismissal of client 04
> Client withdrawn by family
>   without staff approval 05
> Client withdrawn by family
>   with staff approval 06
> Referred 07
> Moved 08
> Incarcerated 09
> Death 10
> Transfer 11

19. Patterns of Drug Use at Admission—

Frequency of Use Prior to Admission:		Severity of Problem:
0=No use mo. prior	4=Once daily	0=Use not a problem
1=Less than 1/wk	5=2-3X's/day	1=Primary
2=Once/wk	6=More than	2=Secondary
3=Several X's/wk	3X's/day	3=Tertiary

	Frequency	Severity
Heroin	0 1 2 3 4 5 6	0 1 2 3
Illegal Meth	0 1 2 3 4 5 6	0 1 2 3
Other opiates	0 1 2 3 4 5 6	0 1 2 3
Alcohol	0 1 2 3 4 5 6	0 1 2 3
Barbiturates	0 1 2 3 4 5 6	0 1 2 3
Other sedatives	0 1 2 3 4 5 6	0 1 2 3
Amphetamines	0 1 2 3 4 5 6	0 1 2 3
Cocaine	0 1 2 3 4 5 6	0 1 2 3
Marijuana/Hash	0 1 2 3 4 5 6	0 1 2 3
Hallucinogens	0 1 2 3 4 5 6	0 1 2 3
Inhalants	0 1 2 3 4 5 6	0 1 2 3
Over-the-counter	0 1 2 3 4 5 6	0 1 2 3
Tranquilizers	0 1 2 3 4 5 6	0 1 2 3
PCP	0 1 2 3 4 5 6	0 1 2 3
Other _____	0 1 2 3 4 5 6	0 1 2 3

When you contact the client, use something similar to the following introduction:

> I am _____, an interviewer from (name of agency). According to our records, you completed our program about three months ago. We are calling to get your ideas on aspects of the program that could be improved and on factors that you thought were strong points. The information you provide will be kept confidential. The people you had (as counselors, representing you, helping you, or other appropriate description) will never be able to connect you with anything you might say. The information you provide will be combined with that provided by other people and presented in summary form only.

20. I would like to start off with some questions about your (counselor or other appropriate description). Would you say that your (counselor/_____) was hard to talk with nearly always, some of the time, or hardly ever?

                                    Nearly always 1
                                    Some of the time .. 2
                                    Hardly ever 3
                              .   Don't know 8
                                    Refused 9

21. Did your (counselor) understand you nearly always, some of the time, or hardly ever?

                                    Nearly always 1
                                    Some of the time .. 2
                                    Hardly ever 3
                                    Don't know 8
                                    Refused 9

22. Would you say that your (counselor) was very helpful, somewhat helpful, or not too helpful?

                                    Very helpful 1
                                    Somewhat helpful .. 2
                                    Not too helpful 3
                                    Don't know 8
                                    Refused 9

23. I would like you to think back on your experiences at (name of agency) and tell me one or two things that you felt were weaknesses in the program.

    _____ ____
    _____ ____

24. Now I would like you to tell me about one or two of the program's strong points.

————————————————————————   ————
————————————————————————   ————

25. Next, I would like to know how you have been getting along since you finished at (agency). Have you been working since you finished?

                                            Yes 1
                    Skip to question 26   [No 2
                                            [Refused .. 9

A. Are you working now?

                                            Yes 1
                    Skip to question 26   [No 2
                                            [Refused .. 9

   1. Do you feel better about your work now than before you started treatment?

                                    Yes 1
                                    No 2
                                    Did not work before .. 7
                                    Refused 9

   2. How long have you had your present job?

                                    WEEKS ... ————
                                    Refused 999

   3. How many hours a week do you work?

                                    HOURS ... ——
                                    Refused 99

4. Does your current job pay more or involve more responsibility than the jobs you have had before?

More pay 1
More responsibility 2
More pay and responsibility ... 3
Neither 4
Did not work before 7
Refused 9

26. Have you gone to school since you have finished at (name of agency)?

Skip to question 27

Yes 1
No 2
Refused .. 9

A. How many weeks did you attend?

WEEKS ... ____
Refused 999

B. Are you still going to school, did you finish the program, stop going, or what?

Still going to school ... 1
Finished program 2
Stopped going 3
Other 4
Refused 9

27. How have you been getting along with your friends since you finished at (agency)? Would you say very well, pretty well, or not too well?

Very well 1
Pretty well 2
Not too well 3
Don't have friends ... 4
Don't know 8
Refused 9

28.   How about with your parents? Would you say you have been getting along with them very well, pretty well, or not at all?

Very well 1
Pretty well 2
Not too well 3
Don't see them 4
No parents 7
Don't know 8
Refused 9

29.   Since you finished at (agency), how would you say you have been getting along with men/women? Would you say very well, pretty well, or not too well?

Very well 1
Pretty well 2
Not too well 3
Don't have contact
  with appropriate
  sex 4
Don't know 8
Refused 9

30.   Since leaving (agency), would you say you are angry or tense most of the time, some of the time, or once in a while?

Most of the time ... 1
Some of the time .. 2
Once in a while ... 3
Never 4
Don't know 8
Refused 9

31. Since leaving (agency), would you say you are depressed or unhappy most of the time, some of the time, or once in a while?

> Most of the time ... 1
> Some of the time .. 2
> Once in a while ... 3
> Never 4
> Don't know 8
> Refused 9

32. Have you been in trouble with the law since you finished at (agency)?

> Yes 1
> No 2
> Don't know ... 8
> Refused 9

33. Have you used any alcohol since you finished at (agency)?

> Yes 1
> Skip to question 34 ⌈ No 2
> ⌊ Refused .. 9

   A. How many times have you used alcohol during the last four weeks?

> Less than once/week 01
> Once per week 02
> Several times per week 03
> Once daily 04
> Two or three times per day .. 05
> More than 3 times per day ... 06
> None in last 4 weeks 07
> Don't know 98
> Refused 99

34. Have you used marijuana since you finished at (agency)?

Yes 1

Skip to question 35   ⎡ No 2
                        ⎣ Refused .. 9

A. How many times have you used marijuana during the last four weeks?

Less than once per week 01
Once per week 02
Several times per week 03
Once daily 04
Two to three times per day .. 05
More than 3 times per day ... 06
None in last four weeks 07
Don't know 98
Refused 99

35. Have you used any other drugs since you finished at (agency)?

Yes 1

Skip to question 36   ⎡ No 2
                        ⎣ Refused .. 9

A. What kind? _____

B. How many times have you used other drugs during the last four weeks?

Less than once per week 01
Once per week 02
Several times per week 03
Once daily 04
Two to three times per day .. 05
More than 3 times per day ... 06
None in last four weeks 07
Don't know 98
Refused 99

36. Is there anything else you could tell me that would help to improve the (agency) program?

Yes ... 1
No ... 2

_____
_____
_____
_____

Thank you very much for your help.

To be Completed Immediately After the Interview—

37. Overall, how great was the respondent's interest in the interview?

Very high 1
Above average 2
Average 3
Below average 4

38. How suspicious did the respondent seem about the interview before you began?

Not at all 1
Somewhat 2
Very suspicious ... 3

39. How would you assess the reliability of the data obtained?

Excellent 1
Good 2
Fair 3
Poor 4
Worthless 5

40. How would you assess the degree of cooperation given by the respondent?

Very cooperative .. 1
Cooperative 2
Neutral 3
Reluctant 4
Hostile 5

41. Anything else about the respondent or the interview that seems important?

_____

_____

_____

REMOVE TRACKING RECORD AFTER CHECKING TO MAKE SURE INTERVIEW SCHEDULE IS COMPLETED.

ASSESSING OTHER OUTCOMES

There are numerous outcomes the sample interview does not tap. Measures for other outcomes are available from a variety of sources. For many human services, professional associations have devised measures for use in national surveys. We strongly recommend that these measures be used. They were probably developed by experts and have been thoroughly tested. If your national association has not developed measures, urge them to undertake such studies.

The next option is to search out sources of interview items. One of the best sources is a publication entitled *Monitoring the Outcomes of Social Services* by Miller, Hatry, and Ross (1977), which may be purchased from the Urban Institute, 2100 M Street, N.W., Washington, D.C., 20037.

The last resort is to devise and test your own questions. This is by far the most difficult and should not be attempted without professional help. Sociologists and political scientists at your local college or university who do survey research may be willing to volunteer a few hours of assistance. Because researchers measure things in great detail for their own studies, you may be deluged by more questions than you need. Select the ones that are the most direct and simple and test them on a group of approximately forty clients. The researcher who devised the questions can tell you what to look for in making the final selection. Briefly, what one looks for is (1) whether most clients answer the question (with something other than don't know or unrelated materials) and (2) whether there is variability in the responses (some people select every answer category). If both these criteria are met, the item is probably safe to use. Finally, if responses seem to correlate with other outcomes in a way you expect, the question is probably a good candidate for long-term use.

The list of items below is not inclusive or complete. Most have been tried in other studies and are probably reliable indicators. Nevertheless, they should probably be tested on a small group of clients before use. If they have to be modified in any way, they should definitely be tested.

Income and Economic Factors

During the last three months, did you or any other member of your household receive income from—

	Yes	No	DK	REF
Unemployment	1	2	8	9
Worker's Compensation	1	2	8	9
Medicaid	1	2	8	9
Social Security	1	2	8	9
Rent Support	1	2	8	9
Food Stamps	1	2	8	9
Welfare	1	2	8	9

Since you left (agency), has your financial situation been getting better, getting worse, or has it stayed the same?

Getting better 1
Getting worse 2
Stayed the same ..3
Don't Know......8
Refused.........9

Marital Instability

Even people who get along with their spouse sometimes wonder whether their marriage is working out. Have you thought your marriage might be in trouble?

Yes..............1

No..............2

Has the thought of getting a divorce or separation crossed your mind since leaving the program?

Yes..............1

No..............2

Have you discussed divorce or separation with a close friend?

Yes..............1

No..............2

Have you or your husband/wife ever seriously suggested the idea of divorce since you left the program?

Yes..............1

No..............2

Did you talk about consulting an attorney?

Yes..............1

No..............2

Comparing your marriage around the time you left (agency), is your marriage getting better, staying the same, or getting worse?

Getting better 1

Staying the same...2

Getting worse 3

Physical Limitations and Health

Do you have any health or physical condition that limits you in dressing, bathing, eating, working, or keeping house?

Yes..............1

No..............2

IF YES, PROBE TO FIT INTO ONE OF THESE 5 CATEGORIES:

Require help in dressing, bathing, or eating and not able to work or keep house at all 1

Able to dress, bathe, and feed myself, but not able to work or keep house at all 2

Able to work or keep house, but limited in the amount or kind of work or housework 3

Able to work or keep house, but limited in kind or amount of other activities such as shopping or exercise................4

Not limited in any of the above ways........................5

Do you have a physical or health condition that restricts your ability to move about or use transportation facilities?

Yes..............1

No..............2

IF YES, PROBE AND FIT INTO ONE OF THESE 4 CATEGORIES:

Must stay in bed all or most of the time 1

Must stay in the house all or most of the time or need human assistance to go outside 2

Able to go outside alone, but required assistance to use automobile or public transportation 3

Able to drive or use public transportation by myself 4

Do you require any mechanical aids to walk or move about?

Yes..............1

No..............2

IF YES, PROBE AND FIT INTO ONE OF THESE CATEGORIES:

Must stay in bed or chair most of the day 1

Able to propel self alone in a wheelchair 2

Able to walk, but must use a cane, crutches, or a mechanical aid, limited in lifting, stooping, or using stairs, limited in speed or distance I can walk...........................3

Walk freely with no limitation of any kind 4

Were there any days during the past two weeks that you cut down on your activities because you were sick?

Yes..............1

No..............2

During the past year, have you had any health problems or illnesses that you have had for more than three months?

Yes..............1

No..............2

Have you seen a doctor during the last twelve months since leaving the program)?

Yes..............1

No..............2

When you compare your health now to what it was after you stopped receiving help from (agency), would you say it is not better, about the same, or worse?

Better 1
About the same...2
Worse 3

Child Problems

Since you left (agency), how often has (name of child) had tantrums? Would you say frequently, occasionally, or hardly ever?

Frequently 1
Occasionally 2
Hardley ever 3

Stole things from others?

Frequently 1
Occasionally 2
Hardly ever 3

Refused to do what was asked?

Frequently 1
Occasionally 2
Hardly ever 3

Played hooky?

Frequently 1
Occasionally 2
Hardly ever 3

Destroyed property?

Frequently 1
Occasionally 2
Hardly ever 3

Was withdrawn?

Frequently 1
Occasionally 2
Hardly ever 3

Physically hurt others?

Frequently 1
Occasionally 2
Hardly ever 3

Run away from home?

Frequently 1
Occasionally 2
Hardly ever 3

Been in trouble with law?

Frequently 1

Occasionally 2

Hardly ever 3

When comparing your child's behavior now with what it was when you left (agency), would you say it is now better, about the same, or worse?

Better 1

About the same... 2

Worse 3

Client Perception of Outcome—General questions

Considering the problems that led you to get help from (agency), how would you say things are now? Would you say they are better, worse, or about the same?

Better 1

Worse 2

About the same... 3

A. Would you say that (agency) contributed to this change a great deal, somewhat, or very little?

A great deal 1

Somewhat 2

Very little........ 3

CONFIDENTIALITY OF CLIENT INFORMATION

It is, of course, imperative that information about the client's responses remain completely confidential. To help maintain confidentiality, we ask persons interviewing clients to sign the agreement below. This is especially vital if volunteers are being used to supplement staff on the follow-up study.

Name of Agency

Agreement for Follow-up Study Interviewers

I, _____ , as an interviewer for the Follow Up Study, being conducted by (agency), agree to the following conditions:

1. I have read the confidentiality statement;
2. I have read the "Procedures for Tracking Former Clients" and "Interviewing Instructions";
3. I agree to follow the procedures as stated in no. 2 above;

4. I agree to strictly maintain the confidentiality of any and all client information that I should acquire as part of my work in the follow up study.

Signature_____ Date_____
Name_____ Witness_____

ANALYZING COMPLETED INTERVIEWS

The interview schedule is set up for computer or hand analysis of the data. For computer analysis, the card and column numbers should be inserted in the right-hand margin of the interview schedule before it is printed. Data, then, can be entered directly into the computer from the completed schedules and analyzed using almost any type of software. Those inexperienced with the use of computers should get help in assigning code, column, and card numbers, entering the data into the computer, and analyzing the data.

For those who will be doing a hand tabulation, we have more detailed instructions. The *first step* is to number each interview schedule in the upper right hand corner using a four digit number beginning with 0001. This is an identification number that will allow one to check between various tabulations and the analyses. Indentification numbers should be assigned at the time the interview is completed so that the exact number of interviews that have been completed is known at any given time. The identification number also helps to prevent the schedule from being misfiled.

The *second step* is to transfer information from the interview schedule to the Tabulation Form at regular intervals. Monthly is a good regimen to get into. The Tabulation Form allows one to collect information from a large number of interviews on a few pages. In collected form, the data is easier to use when compiling summary reports. The sample tabulation form on the following page helps to summarize information for monthly and annual reports. It includes information from those items on the interview schedule needed to generate a report. A different tabulation form can be derived to aid in the preparation of other types of reports, or a single tabulation form may be used as the basis of several reports.

Note that the Tabulation Form carries a description of each item in the left hand margin as well as the question number. This reduces errors when data is being transferred as well as when reports are being compiled.

When transferring information to the Tabulation Form, record the exact figure or the number that is circled on the interview schedule. For example, if the number 3 is circled in answer to question 11 (employment at conclusion of treatment), a 3 is entered in the square in the third row of the Tabulation Form in the column for that particular interview. Enter all information from a particular interview schedule before proceeding to the next one.

Each time data is summarized from the Tabulation Form, a note should be made above the identification number where the last summarization stopped. That way, one can build on previous compilations and not have to recompile old data. Tabulation Form pages should be numbered to avoid mix ups.

The *third step* is to summarize the information into a report. We devised a form that can be used both as a worksheet to summarize the information and as summary table to present the

Page Number _____

Tabulation of Follow-up Study Data

Identification Number										
Age 1										
Employment at conclusion of treatment 11										
Employment during treatment 14										
Employment since treatment Any 25										
Current 25A										
Pay and Responsibility 25A.4										

Education during treatment 13											
Education since treatment 26											
Continuing 26A											
In trouble with law before treatment 4											
In trouble with law after treatment 32											
Prior treatment 3											
Termination 18											
Alcohol—severity of prior use 19											
Extent of use prior 19											
Extent of use after treatment 33A											
Marijuana—severity of prior use 19											
Extent of use prior to treatment 19											
Extent of use after treatment 34A											
Other drugs—severity of prior use 19											
Extent of use prior to treatment 19											
Extent of use after treatment 35B											

information. A summary form completed as a worksheet is included in this chapter.

We elected to summarize information about employment, schooling, legal problems, alcohol use, marijuana, and other drug use. These broad categories are listed in the left-hand margin of the summary form, along with the subcategories under each heading. The number in parentheses following each subcategory identifies the interview schedule item number and the subcategory that is to be summarized. For example, the numbers following the "Employed" category is 11-2,3, which indicates that interview respondents who have a 2 (employed part-time at conclusion of treatment) or 3 (employed full-time at the conclusion of treatment) next to item 11 on the Tabulation Form are to be considered here. For each person in that category, you look at items 25 and 25A on the Tabulation Form. If they have a 1 in both items, make a tic (/) next to the "worked continuously since treatment" category on the Summary Form. If they have a 1 for item 25 and a 2 for item 25A, make a tic next the "worked but now unemployed" category. If they have a 2 for item 25, mark a tic next to the "not worked since treatment" category. Go through and tic off the remainder of the categories on the Summary Form for that completed interview. When you get to alcohol, marijuana, and drug use, you are comparing present and past treatment levels and marking the category of change. For example, if they have a 4 on extent of alcohol prior to treatment (item 19 on Tabulation Form) and a 2 on use after treatment (item 33A on Tabulation Form), place a tic next to "decrease of two or more levels" on the Summary Form. If information is missing for any category on the Tabulation Form, simply omit the case from the summary.

Once the information from the Tabulation Form has been recorded on the Summary Form, the tics may be counted and the totals recorded. Calculate percentages by dividing the numbers in each category by the total number for which there is information. The table may be done over on a new Summary Form, omitting tic's and other extraneous information for presentation as a report.

You may find it useful to make separate summaries for subgroups of clients such as those who completed the program successfully, stayed in the program for an extended period, received a particular form of treatment or service, were treated by

more skilled staff, etc. Such summaries can tell you about the
strengths and weaknesses of your program, which can then be
used for the variety of planning and administrative purposes
described earlier.

Summary of Follow-up Interviews
Date _____

Number of completed interviews   146

	Frequency	*Percent*
Employment at conclusion of treatment		
Employed (11-2,3)*		
Worked continuously since treatment (25-1/25A-1) ~~HHT HHT HHT HHT~~ ~~HHT HHT HHT~~ III	38	58
Worked but now unemployed (25-1/25A-2) ~~HHT HHT HHT~~ I	16	25
Not worked since treatment (25-2) ~~HHT HHT~~ I	11	17
	65	100
Unemployed (11-1)		
Worked continuously since treatment (25-1/25A-1) ~~HHT HHT~~ I	11	13
Worked but now unemployed (25-1/25A-2) ~~HHT HHT~~ I	11	13
Not worked since treatment (25-2) ~~HHT HHT HHT HHT HHT HHT HHT~~ ~~HHT HHT HHT HHT HHT HHT~~	65	74
	87	100
Education obtained during treatment		
Went to school during treatment (13-2,3)		
Continued education after treatment (26-1) ~~HHT HHT HHT HHT HHT HHT~~ ~~HHT HHT HHT HHT HHT~~ II	57	69
Did not continue education after treatment (26-2) ~~HHT HHT HHT HHT HHT~~ I	26	31
	83	100

---

*First number in parentheses refers to interview schedule item number, and numbers following hyphen refer to response code.

Summary (Continued)

	Frequency	Percent
Did not go to school during treatment (13-1)		
Went to school after treatment (26-1) ~~HHT HHT HHT~~ II	17	27
Did not go to school after treatment (26-2) ~~HHT HHT HHT HHT HHT~~ ~~HHT HHT HHT HHT~~ I	46	73
	63	100

Legal Status

	Frequency	Percent
In trouble with the law prior to treatment (4-2)		
In trouble with the law since treatment (32-1) ~~HHT HHT HHT HHT~~ III ~~HHT HHT HHT HHT~~	43	38
Not in trouble with the law since treatment (32-2) ~~HHT HHT HHT HHT HHT HHT HHT~~ I ~~HHT HHT HHT HHT HHT HHT HHT~~	71	62
	114	100

	Frequency	Percent
No history of problem before treatment (4-1)		
In trouble with the law since treatment (32-1) ~~HHT~~	5	17
Not in trouble with the law since treatment (32-2) ~~HHT HHT HHT HHT HHT~~ II	27	83
	32	100

Drug use since treatment for clients for whom alcohol use was primary, secondary, or tertiary before treatment (19-4)

	Frequency	Percent
No use in four weeks prior to follow-up interview (33-2/33A-7) ~~HHT HHT HHT~~ I	16	16
Decrease of two levels or more† (33A) ~~HHT HHT~~ ~~HHT~~ I	16	16
Decrease of one level (33A) ~~HHT HHT HHT~~ ~~HHT HHT~~ II	27	26
Same or worse use (33A) ~~HHT HHT HHT HHT~~ IIII ~~HHT HHT HHT HHT~~	44	42
	103	100

Marijuana use was primary, secondary,
or tertiary problem before treatment
(19-9)

No use in four weeks prior to follow-
up interview (34-2/34A-7) ‖‖‖‖‖‖‖‖‖‖‖‖‖‖‖‖II   32   26
Decrease of two levels or more (34A) ‖‖‖‖‖‖‖‖‖I 21   17
Decrease of one level (34A) ‖‖‖‖‖‖‖‖‖I   21   17
Same or worse use (34A) ‖‖‖‖‖‖‖‖‖‖‖‖‖‖‖‖‖I   _26_   _40_
                                                      124   100

Another type of drug was primary,
secondary, or tertiary problem before
treatment (19-1, 2, 3, 5, 6, 7, 8, 10, 11, 12
13, 14, 15)

No use in four weeks prior to follow-
up interview (35-2/35B-7) ‖‖‖‖‖‖‖‖‖‖‖‖‖‖‖‖‖‖‖‖‖‖‖‖‖‖‖‖ 54   67
Decrease of two or more levels (35B)   ‖‖‖‖
Decrease of one level (35B) ‖‖‖‖‖‖‖I   11   13
Same or worse use (35B) ‖‖‖‖‖‖‖‖‖‖‖I   _16_   _20_
                                                      81   100

---

†Use levels
1—Less than once/week
2—Once/week
3—Several times/week
4—Once daily
5—2 to 3 times/day
6—More than 3 times/day

RECOMMENDATIONS FOR FUNDING
ORGANIZATION ADMINISTRATORS

Agencies should be given every encouragement to do follow-up
studies of clients. Too few agencies conduct such studies, even
though outcome information is a powerful evaluation and
management tool. Some agency executives are reluctant to collect
such information, because they fear that if the information is
unfavorable, it may be used against them. Assurances that such

information will generally be used to build and improve services may help to reduce apprehension. Other agency executives are reluctant to collect follow-up information, because it is something they have never done before and are uncertain how to get underway. Offers of help and reference materials may help to surmount resistance caused by inexperience.

To encourage agencies to do follow-up studies, call attention to the ones that have. Let it be known they are doing good work and represent a model other agencies should emulate. The agency doing the follow-up gets a pat on the back, while others are encouraged to undertake such studies.

A follow-up study that reveals that less than a majority of clients improve their condition as a result of participation in the program is not cause for alarm. It may reflect the "state of the art." If similar agencies report comparable results, such an explanation seems reasonable. If, on the other hand, a particular agency's success rate is lower than that of other agencies, creative efforts to improve service delivery may be indicated. Funding organization staff should keep in mind that the limited success may be due to under funding.

Outcome information is excellent data to report to constituents such as taxpayers and donors as well as to the next higher level of administration. So much of the impact of human service work must be taken as an article of faith that simple outcome information is often a welcomed addition. Some information is better than none, and it encourages decision making based on fact rather than guesswork.

Hard information on outcomes can help in calculating some of the costs and benefits of human service programs. Some information is already available of the costs of letting certain problems go unattended. Outcome information can help to assess the extent to which these costs can be averted by human service programs.

Finally, funding organizations should make use of outcome information in their funding decisions. Nothing discourages evaluation more than to have painstakingly gathered information ignored in making crucial funding decisions. The way outcome information can be effectively used in funding decisions is described in detail in Chapter 4.

ALLOCATING FEWER RESOURCES IN THE FACE OF ESCALATING REQUESTS
A Guide for Funding Organization Administrators

INTRODUCTION

In times of decreasing resources, organizations receive increasing pressure from two sources. On the one hand, donors, and particularly taxpayers, press for more accountability. They are more selective about where they want their dollars spent, and they want the money spent on programs that are efficient. In times of scarce resources, these demands are difficult to resist. On the other hand, funding organizations are pressured more effectively by human services agencies seeking the limited resources. Not only do human service executives make more convincing cases that are backed by hard evidence, but they are more skilled in lobbying on behalf of their cause. These cross pressures, coupled by more limited funds to allocate, mean that funders often find themselves having to make hard choices. Funding organizations can no longer "give some" to everybody. Nor can they routinely fund agencies they have been helping for years or even decades. Hard choices must be made between popular programs such as emergency assistance to those out of work, recreation programs sponsored by traditional groups, and effective delinquency prevention programs operated by new (and perhaps militant) neighborhood organizations. In short, in hard times, funding organizations are the objects of strong cross pressures that create difficult decisions.

Given these conditions, the funding organization must have an allocation process that is flexible, relies on well-understood criteria, and commands respect. Moreover, the process must be able to accommodate change. There has to be a way to fund programs that meet changing and emerging needs and to reduce funding for programs judged to be of low priority or that are operating inefficiently. In addition, funding decisions need to be based on a widely accepted set of criteria that are known to the applicant as well as taxpayers and donors. Finally, the decision-making group and the procedures they use to allocate funds must be respected and judged to be fair. If the funding process meets these standards, the cross pressures become useful inputs rather than acrimonious exchanges, law suits, and adverse publicity. The allocation processes outlined as follows are ones that help achieve these objectives.

In the paragraphs that follow, the authors suggest ways the review group should be put together to enhance the credibility of the funding decisions. This is followed by an overview of the central components of the application review process. Special attention is given to the information needed to reach decisions and the process of devising and using criteria to evaluate the information. The authors conclude with a discussion of the need for conflict of interest policy, the powers of the funding organization, and recommendations for agency executives.

COMPOSITION OF THE REVIEW GROUP

Most elected groups (city councils or county boards) that consider human service funding consist of a small number of individuals who must deal with so many matters that human services often do not receive a thorough review. Groups of elected officials could benefit from human service planning groups similar to those established in many cities for land use planning. Human service planning groups could aid elected officials by conducting agency evaluations (*see* Chapter 5), establishing human service priorities (*see* Chapter 6), establishing criteria for evaluating fund applications, and actually rating applications and making recommendations to elected officials. The way in which one such advisory group came into being and operates is described in Chapter Seven.

For United Way, the use of volunteers in reaching funding decisions is traditional, so that the composition of the review group is a vital question. The groups responsible for funding decisions in foundations vary extensively from organization to organization. Sometimes only a small number of staff are involved. Because foundations are more insulated from the cross pressures described above, review group composition may not be such a crucial issue. But it may become so in the future as more and more pressure is applied to gain access to the funds.

The first matter to consider is the number of people needed for funding decisions. In using volunteers, we found that a team of nine people could review the applications of three human services agencies over a two-month period. With this assignment, the group was pretty much stretched to the limit. Thus, to review 24 agencies would require 72 volunteers. Establishing priorities and conducting program evaluations was handled by different groups of volunteers.

Staggered terms for review groups members is essential to insure continuity. Volunteers are usually good for two to three years of service on a given project. This rate of turnover means that recruiting and training is a fairly constant process. Planned turnover is an advantage, however, in that it keeps the process open and prevents donors, taxpayers, and applicants from feeling that an "old boy network" is making all the decisions. The new blood brought in as a result of turnover also keeps the review group more responsive to changes in human service needs.

Recruiting people from diverse backgrounds is also essential to keeping the review process open and balanced. Given the diversity of human services, it is important to recruit from business, labor, the professions, the minority community, women, and different regions of the community. Recruiting people with accounting skills who understand a balance sheet is vital for a thorough line item analysis of the budget. People who have served on boards and in other volunteer capacities for a variety of human service organizations are also invaluable. Such persons are in a good position to make the interagency comparisons so vital when resources are scarce.

ORGANIZATION OF THE REVIEW PROCESS

Given the number and diversity of people reviewing applications and the complexity of the task, training and orientation are important. Through training, the review group becomes familiar with the process, the application forms, and the criteria upon which decisions are to be based. Examples of applications that would get high ratings and some that would receive low ones should be presented. A training session of four hours (or two two-hour sessions) should be sufficient. A manual summarizing the review process is essential and can be the point around which training revolves.

Those reviewing the funding requests are not the only group requiring orientation. Applicants also need information and guidelines for making application. Most forms are complex, and what the reviewers want is not always clear from written guidelines. Step-by-step instructions are needed for first-time applicants, and veterans need reminders and information on changes in the form. All applicants need information on the criteria that will be used in evaluating the applications. An orientation session for applicants should also include instructions on how to link budgets to goals and objectives and how to estimate expenses and income. Orientation meetings also serve to keep an open dialogue between funders and agencies to clear up misunderstandings and other matters not easily handled in memos and correspondence.

The basic document in the funding process is the application. The form should have provisions for obtaining all of the information needed to reach a decision. Since no form is perfect, and applicants are not equally thorough in providing information, we also recommend a site visit or budget presentation to supplement the application. This gives members of the review group an opportunity to ask questions, and applicants have a chance to reinforce certain points and communicate things they may not want to put in writing.

To expedite the site visits or budget presentation, we recommend that the questions the review group has be written and transmitted to the agency executive at least a week in advance. This allows the applicant to assemble and present the best information available. Moreover, it reduces the chance of the applicant being caught by surprise and leaving the budget presentation or site visit frustrated and perhaps embarrassed.

Agency executives should be encouraged to reply in writing so that the reviewers have something to which to refer when deciding on a recommendation.

Between the site visit and the budget presentation, the site visit is superior. While more time-consuming, review groups that make site visits gain vast quantities of information about the clients, program, staff, maintenance, and facilities that just cannot be obtained in any other way. Details can be obtained from a brief look around that can never be gleaned from application forms or executive testimony.

Soon after the site visit or budget presentation (preferably immediately after, when the information is still fresh), recommendations are formulated. Recommendations should be based on (1) a line item analysis of the budget that adjusts the request for inaccuracies and brings it into conformity with funding agency rules, and (2) the application of criteria on the need for and effectiveness of the program. After preliminary decisions are finalized by the funding agency, they are sent to the agency.

Agencies should have an opportunity to appeal the recommendation where they feel the decision did not take into account all of the facts or was flawed by errors in the review goup's analysis. Finally, the fundi..g organization should review its application form, site visit or hearing procedures, criteria, and decision-making processes at the close of each year to see if they can be streamlined or made more responsive.

INFORMATION NEEDED TO MAKE FUNDING DECISIONS

Often members of review groups propose that requests for this or that bit of information should be added to the application because it would make their task easier. Then, agency executives sometimes take the approach of presenting an abundance of information in the hopes of appealing to every member of the review group. It is easy for the applications to end in information overload, giving members of review groups too much information to process, and at the same time complicating the agency executive's life by demanding information that is seldom used.

For both parties, it is helpful to put limits on the length of the answers that applicants can give, and to review annually each item of data requested and prune out those items not used by most of the members of the review group.

Listed below are items of information essential to conducting a thorough and fair review of fund applications. In some cases, the text of questions needed to solicit the information is given, as are examples of high quality answers. Specific budget categories and forms are not suggested, as requirements vary from community to community. The sequence in which the items are presented is the order in which a new reviewer might want to see them. The authors begin with categories of information needed to review programs that have been funded before. At the end of the section, items of information needed when considering an agency for the first time are presented.

We make the assumption that the applications are for particular programs and not for agency support in general. Funding by program is essential to controlling expenses and having better knowledge of how the money is spent. In short, program funding is essential for efficiency and accountability.

STRUCTURE OF AGENCY REQUESTING FUNDS.   To put the request for program funds in context, it is useful to obtain information on the agency itself. The purpose of the agency can be obtained from the answer to the item: "In a paragraph of no more than 250 words, describe the purpose of the agency. Indicate the specific problems the agency is intended to alleviate and list the programs in operation to bring about the change." Additional information can be gleaned from asking the agency to include an organization chart. Information on the governing board may be gained by a few simple questions about the number of members, principal committees, and the frequency of meetings. Some funding organizations like to see a list of the board members with their office, address, occupation, years of service, and term expiration date. If representation is something the funding organization wants to monitor, questions about the proportion of the board that is female, minority, under thirty, over sixty, and residing in the service area can be asked. If the review group wants to tap inbreeding, the following question would be helpful: "How many of your current board members have served five consecutive years or longer?" This question gives the reviewers information on whether the programs are within the mainstream of the agency's operation and how the program is governed.

RECENT HISTORY OF THE PROGRAM. It is difficult to make funding decisions without knowing about changes that have been occurring in recent years. The following suggests a way that information on funding, staff, volunteers, and services can be obtained. From this information, the reviewer has an opportunity to assess changes in the effectiveness of the program (see Chapter 2 for details on making use of such information) as well as funding and staff problems and strengths.

1. Recent history is an important factor in making funding decisions, in developing program plans, and in evaluating program accomplishments. Please complete the following four-year summary form:

A. Source of Funds	1981 Dollars	%	1982 Dollars	%	1983 Dollars	%	1984 (Proposed) Dollars	%
United Way								
County								
City of								
State of								
Federal Payments								
Foundations								
User Fees								
Other								
TOTALS								

B. Staff Assigned
   to Program (FTE)*

Administration				
Professional				
Support				
TOTALS				

*For example: 1.5 FTE = 1 Employee working 2,080 hrs./yr. and
                1 Employee working 1,040 hrs./yr.

C. Volunteers

Number of Volunteers				
Full-Time Equivalency*				

D. Amount of Service Provided

First, provide the number of *unduplicated* clients served. Second, list the number of units of service provided and the unit of service definition. The definition should not change from one year to the next. If more than one unit of service is used, list each with a separate definition.

	1981	1982	1983	1984
Number of Unduplicated Clients				

Number of Units of Service				

Definition:

Number of Units of Service				

Definition:

Number of Units of Service				

Definition:

---

*For example: 1.5 FTE = 1 Employee working 2,080 hrs./yr. and
                1 Employee working 1,040 hrs./yr.

Number of Units of Service				

Definition:

Number of Units of Service				

Definition:

MISSION OF THE PROGRAM.   It is important for reviewers to have a specific idea of what the program staff are trying to accomplish and the services they are providing to try and achieve their purpose. Agency executives often (usually unintentionally) state their mission in vague terms or ones so full of jargon that the nonprofessional has trouble understanding. To help avoid this, the mission question should be very specific. Consider the following example:

> In a paragraph of no more than 250 words, describe the purpose of the program. Indicate the specific problems the program is intended to alleviate and the methods (approach) that are used to bring about the change. Be specific about the target population and the changes you wish to bring about in this population as a result of the services rendered. Do not use vague terms, such as "increase quality of life" or "help people achieve self-fulfillment." If possible, state the changes the program is intended to bring about in measurable (numerical) terms.

The following is a sample answer to the question that reviewers would find useful. Notice that the answer is very specific. It states who the program is designed for, the problems the program is trying to treat, and the methods being used to achieve their objective.

The Personal Adjustment program is designed to help adolescents from 10 to 20 years of age shift from one stage of development to another with a minimum of stress. The stages we deal with most frequently are the development of secondary sexual characteristics (puberty), decline in dependence on parents, increase in influence of peers, and development of post-high-school work and education plans. By easing the transition, we hope to increase the extent to which adolescents get along with their parents, families, and members of the opposite sex, and to decrease the incidence of depression, feelings of anger, drug or alcohol misuse, and getting in trouble with the law. The methods we use are individual and group counseling. Usually, the group counseling is oriented around a particular stage of development.

OBJECTIVES FOR THE PERIOD COVERED BY THE REQUEST.   While part of any request is to maintain existing efforts, most administrators try to improve the program. Among other things, they may want to try to serve difficult to reach clients, upgrade staff by training or hiring new people, finetune the administration of the organization, and increase revenues. Most such objectives or goals (we don't distinguish between the two) have consequences for the budget. Either they mean finding new funds or redistributing old ones. In order to fully evaluate a request, reviewers need to know what the program administrator plans to do and how he/she plans to finance it. The following questions tap these changes in specific terms.

List the objectives of the program for *(request year)*. For each objective listed, please specify—

A. The condition or situation you wish to change, as it exists in (current year), stated, if possible, in numerical terms,

B. the extent to which you wish to change the (current year) condition or situation in (request year), stated, if possible, in numerical terms,

C. the activities staff will engage in to bring about the change,

D. the methods and measures that will be used to determine whether the goal has been achieved,

E. the effect the proposed change has on the budget.

There is also the possibility that changes are occurring to the program that have budgetary implications. Sources of funds may be changing; the client population may be increasing or decreasing, or new laws may affect the terms under which the service is provided. Information on changes that are not in the normal course of events is helpful to reviewers and may be tapped with the question: "Is the program now undergoing significant changes that will influence its operation in 19____? If yes, describe, in specific terms, why and how the program is changing and the implications these changes have for the budget?"

REVENUES FOR THE REQUEST PERIOD. This part of the application not only should contain revenues from all sources for the particular program, but for the entire agency, so that the review group can see where the requested funds fit into the operation of the agency. The amount from city, county, state, federal government, United Way, foundations, user fees, fund raising events, members dues, and other sources should be specified. It is helpful to know what proportion of funds support management and what segment support program services. These figures should be provided for one year prior to the current year as well as the request period. All increases and decreases between the current year and the request period should be justified, and the basis for estimating the changes should be specified in detail. Applicants should be asked to provide client fee scales so that when this figure is combined with the number of service units, income from fees can be estimated independently by the review group. Also, reviewers can see whether the agency is charging enough. The firmness of grant funds and revenue generating contractual arrangements should be specified. It is reasonable to ask the applicant to supply copies of letters specifying the arrangements.

EXPENSES FOR THE REQUEST PERIOD. As with revenues, expenses should be shown for the entire agency as well as the program for which funds are being requested. Expenses for salaries, benefits, supplies, telephone, travel, housing, utilities, fees, capital equipment, and other items should be allocated across management and program services. Information should be provided for the previous year, the current year, and the request period. Increases and decreases should be justified and the basis for arriving at these estimates specified. Because the bulk of the expenses for human service agencies are for personnel, it is reasonable to have the applicant provide supplemental information. For example, it is helpful to have a schedule of positions and salaries showing amount paid, annual salary, percent increase in salary, and the amount paid for various benefits for all three years. A functional analysis of each position according to the percent of time (and possibly dollar amounts) allocated to various programs as well as to management is helpful in understanding the request.

PROGRAM EFFECTIVENESS. How well the program is doing relative to recent past performance is vital in determining funding levels. If the program is continuing to grow and improve, higher levels of funding may be warranted. If the program is going through a decline, perhaps fewer resources are called for, unless the decline is directly attributable to lower levels of funding in the recent past. How a program is doing relative to similar programs is another indicator of effectivenes. Some of the many indicators of effectiveness are detailed in Chapter 2. One way to obtain information on effectiveness on the application form is to ask a question similar to the ones below. An example of a suitable answer to the query by the director of a youth counseling program is also given.

Program *effectiveness* can be defined in a number of ways. Included among these are

1. percent of clients who experience the desired outcome as a result of service provided
2. number of units of service rendered per staff member
3. dollars expended per unit of service rendered
4. proportion of staff with appropriate professional training
5. low administrator/staff ratio
6. years of professional experience per staff member
7. percent of total service provided by volunteers

There are others that could be used as well. Using these *or other* indicators that are appropriate to the program, please indicate the following:

A. How the program's effectiveness has changed over the last three years. (Use at least *three* different indicators.)

1. We do a three month follow-up phone interview on clients after they have completed our program. We ask them the same questions in the follow-up as in the initial interview. We get specific information on how they get along, with

parents and others, and whether they have gotten in trouble with the law. Three years ago, when we started the follow-up internally, only 50 percent reported a decline in arguments with their parents. Now, 75 percent report such a decline. We have been focusing on this area and it has had results.

2. The percent of our professional staff with a MA degree in counseling has climbed from 60 percent in 1980 to 80 percent in 1983.

3. As you can see from our budget figures, we are doing more counseling with less money now than we did last year.

B. How the program's effectiveness compares with that of programs similar to your own in other communities or to national standards. (Use at least *one* indicator.)

1. We compare ourselves with similar programs in Madison Wisconsin and Tacoma, Washington. Our cost per client served in 1983 was $230.94, while the cost/client in Madison was $245.33 and in Tacoma, $240.19. As the three cities are demographically and socially similar, we feel we are a very cost effective service.

NEED FOR THE PROGRAM. If the funding organization already has a set of priorities based on need, then it is only a matter of looking to see what priority the applicant has. For information on establishing a set of priorities refer to Chapter 6. If the funding organization has no established priorities based on need, information can be solicited from the applicant. In fact, it is probably a good idea to ask for such information even where a system of priorities is in place. A program executive may have convincing reasons for dispensing with the priority system, and rigid adherence to a priority system does not always take into account the complex nature of human service needs. The authors recommend the following questions be used to obtain information on need. A sample answer of good quality is also shown.

What is the number of persons needing this program?
15,871 or 1,587 per year

A. How did you arrive at the figure listed above?

Using 1980 census figures, I added together the number of

young people who would be from 10 to 20 years of age in 1984. This figure was multiplied by 54 percent, the projections of youth that our professional society estimates to have transition problems severe enough to require intervention sometime during their adolescence.

B. In the next two years, do you anticipate that the number of people in need of this program will:

    ____ Decrease by _2_ %
    ____ Stay the Same
    ____ Increase by ___ %

C. Briefly explain how you arrived at the preceding response.

Using the 1980 census data, I calculated the number of young people who would be in the target population age in 1985 and 1986 and multiplied by 54 percent, as described previously.

D. What, in specific terms, would be the *effect* upon those persons being served if the program was greatly reduced or not available?

There would be an increase in demand on the psychiatric services of the Community Mental Health Center, and on the various drug and alcohol treatment programs in the community. In addition, the juvenile arrest rate would go up as young people under stress act out against the adult community. The incidence of child abuse would go up as frustrated parents take out their anger on their children.

PAST PERFORMANCE IN RELATION TO FUNDING ORGANIZATION RECOMMENDATIONS. Often awards are made with recommendations that funds be spent in specific ways or that the agency change the way it manages certain fiscal matters, and so on. Information on the executive's compliance with these recommendations should be taken into account in reaching funding decisions. A copy of the preceding year's recommendations should be sent to the agency with the instruction that they indicate how they have dealt with each of the recommendations. Since this may not apply to all applicants, this need not be a part of the application form.

Additional information should be sought from agencies applying for funds to start a new program or to operate a demonstration program. With respect to applicants who have applied before and who are not in trouble, reviewers can safely make the assumption that the staff have the ability to operate the program for another year, that there is a population in need, and that their methods are effective. One cannot make these assumptions about an untested program. Therefore, additional information is needed to make a sound funding decision.

DUPLICATION OF SERVICES. The applicant must be able to show that a need exists that no other agency is serving, although the proposal may be for a program that supplements the services of other agencies. Questions such as the following can be used to elicit the information the agency has gathered. "Who is in need of this program? Be specific about the number of people and the area in which they reside. Describe their mental and physical condition, age, sex, education, minority status, stage in the life cycle, or other characteristics that are appropriate given the type of service the proposed program is to provide. Explain why this population does not now receive the service you propose to provide from other agencies."

EFFECTIVENESS OF METHODS. In cases where the applicant is proposing a new method of providing service or a service that is untried, the reviewers need some assurance that the approach will work. The applicant may be able to cite the experience of other pilot programs, refer to studies that have been conducted, or just make a very convincing argument. Not only is the applicant obligated to show that the new approach will probably work, but provisions must also be made to evaluate the project and find out whether it has been effective. To obtain this information, applicants could be asked to respond to the following questions: "What evidence do you have that the proposed project will be successful? What factors could jeopardize the outcome of the project, and how likely are they to occur? Specifically, how will the success of the project be determined?"

CONTINUATION OF THE PROJECT. If the award is for a demonstration project, there needs to be some evidence the applicant can continue at the conclusion of the funding period. Or, if the applicant is seeking funds from several sources and other funders are giving a one-time-only grant, continuation prospects need to be reviewed. The applicant might be asked, "How will the project be continued after the initial funding period?"

QUALIFICATIONS OF THE APPLICANT.   The applicants have an obligation to show that they have the credentials to conduct the proposed program. Therefore, it is appropriate to ask for vitae or summaries of educational and work experience pertinent to the project. Special questions could be included on the application requesting the agency to demonstrate that the staff are qualified to conduct the proposed project.

CRITERIA TO EVALUATE APPLICATIONS

A line item analysis of the budget of an application can be an effective means of spotting inaccuracies, assessing certain aspects of the management of the program, and identifying fiscal policies that need to be improved. Too often, however, funding organizations get so involved in reviewing the technical aspects of the budget that they ignore many factors that should be taken into account. One reason is that reviewers inexperienced with human service agencies are uncomfortable dealing with such matters as the need for the service and the effectiveness of the program. But, in fairness to the agencies and the taxpayers or donors, funding organizations are obligated to apply a broad set of criteria covering these matters. And, as demands for funds increasingly outdistance the supply, there is an even greater need to take a comprehensive across-programs view of funding. Reallocating funds (cutting some and increasing others) should be done on the basis of criteria that are comprehensive, applied systematically, and understood by applicants, funders, donors, and taxpayers alike.

Formulating criteria and devising procedures for using them should be a task that receives input from a variety of sources. While a committee may put together criteria and suggest a process for using them, the product should be reviewed by a wide cross section of people who are going to review applicantions as well as potential applicants. Comments from these individuals should be obtained before finalizing the process. Once in final form, the criteria and the procedures for using them should be widely publicized. Certainly every applicant should know the criteria and how they are going to be applied. One of the by-products of a systematic use of criteria is that applicants provide better information.

There are many criteria that could be used to evaluate fund applications from human service agencies. The use of three or four oversimplifies a complex operation. Too many criteria (more than a dozen) puts reviewers in the position of making differentiations that are difficult, if not impossible, to make in a meaningful way. The authors propose criteria that funding organizations may find useful as a starting point in developing their own. For each criterion, response categories are suggested that allow reviewers to evaluate complex matters from different points of view. Also, the response categories can be translated into numerical ratings such that the higher the number, the more favorable the application. Following each criterion is a list of the information the reviewers would examine to come up with a rating. The criteria have been listed on a form that might be used by reviewers to record their ratings.

For new programs, the following criteria might be added to the form.

1. To what extent does the proposed program duplicate services available through other programs? (3) No duplication; (2) A small amount of duplication; (1) Considerable duplication? (Review duplication of services information.)

2. To what extent is the proposed approach likely to be an effective means for bringing about the desired impact on the clients? (3) Likely to be effective; (2) Likely to be somewhat effective; (1) Not likely to be effective. (Review effectiveness information.)

3. How good are the prospects for continued funding at the conclusion of grant support? (3) Very good; (2) Pretty good; (1) Not too good. (Review continuation data.)

4. To what extent do the people proposing the project have the skills and experience necessary to organize and operate the proposed project? (3) Highly skilled with proven track

record; (2) Moderately qualified to do proposed project; (1) Limited qualifications to do the project. (Review qualification of applicant.)

PROGRAM RATING WORKSHEET

Agency: _____ Program: _____

After reviewing the application, rate the application on each of the following criteria. Complete these ratings before the meeting and turn them into _____ . Keep a copy for yourself. Make any notes you wish on your own copy only.

Number of
Rating ____

1. To what extent are salary increases and benefits consistent with those requested by similar programs and salary guidelines? (5) A great deal; (4) Considerably; (3) A moderate amount; (2) Very little; (1) Not at all? (Review expenses and salary analysis and guidelines.)   _____

2. To what extent are income projections accurate and realistic? (5) A great deal; (4) Considerably; (3) A moderate amount; (2) Very little; (1) Not at all? (Review revenue projections and objectives for requestion period.)   _____

3. To what extent are projections of expenses accurate, based on sound information, and fully justified? (5) A great deal; (4) Considerably; (3) A moderate amount; (2) Very little; (1) Not at all? (Review expenses and objectives.)   _____

4. To what extent did program management follow last year's recommendations? (5) Fully; (4) Almost entirely; (3) To a moderate degree; (2) Violated a number of recommendations and policies? (Review past performance.)   _____

5. How cost-effective has the program been since the last allocation? (5) Much above average; (4) Above average; (3) Average; (2) Below average; (1) Much below average? (Review effectiveness information and expenses.) _____

6. Overall, how effective is the fiscal planning and management of the program? (5) Much above average; (4) Above average; (3) Average; (2) Below average; (1) Much below average? (Review items 1–5 above.) _____

7. How successful has the program been in providing services since the last allocation relative to previous years? (5) Much above average; (4) Above average; (3) Average; (2) Below average; (1) Much below average? (Review effectiveness information.) _____

8. What is the need for the service provided by the program? (4) Very high; (3) High; (2) Moderate; (1) Low? (Review priority and need for program information.) _____

9. How successful is the program in comparison to other programs of a similar type? (5) Much above average; (4) Above average; (3) Average; (2) Below average; (1) Much below average? (Review effectiveness information.) _____

The reveiw group should evaluate applications after examining the materials, but before meeting to formulate a recommendation. Ratings should be turned into the team leader or a staff member, with review group members keeping a reference copy for themselves. The ratings should be summarized for use at the meeting, where recommendations are formulated. Each member of the review group should receive a copy of the summary. The form on the following page is a model summary sheet. By showing the distribution of the ratings as well as an average rating, the degree of consensus is indicated as well as how the group as a whole feels about the application. The ratings serve to identify (either by the low rating or lack of consensus) problem areas needing further discussion. Review group members should have an opportunity to revise their ratings after deliberations so that the ratings that go forward reflect the evaluation of the reviewers at the time they finalize their funding recommendation.

In addition to serving as a basis for discussion, the ratings may be used in various ways. On the one hand, they may simply be advisory. This gives the review group considerable flexibility in their use of the rating. On the other hand, the ratings could be tied directly to funding. For example, agencies scoring above a certain point could be granted their request after making technical adjustments to the budget. Those falling below would receive no increase or one based on inflation. Or, ratings could be translated into a percentage or dollar increase (or decrease) by the application of a formula. For example, each quarter of a point above the cutoff point could be equivalent to a one percent (or some other unit such as a ½%) increase. Those below would get no increase or even a decrease. It is possible the review group would not want all criteria to carry equal weight. The relative importance of each criteria could be built into the ratings so that a program's allocation could be more heavily based on, say, effectiveness rather than need. To do this, one weights the important criteria by some factor in calculating the overall rating. These are matters for the review group to decide as they gain experience in using the ratings.

Regardless of how the ratings are used, the summary rating should accompany the funding recommendation to groups that review the initial funding recommendation and the transmission of the final recommendation to the applicant. The summary of ratings showing the distribution of the ratings should not be sent forward, as it invites needless second-guessing as to which team members gave which ratings.

Some reviewers may be reluctant to make ratings on things they feel they know little about. For example, one member may feel justified in making a judgment about cost effectiveness, but not on program effectiveness. Other review group members may feel just the reverse. If all team members make the ratings, these factors will balance out in the summary ratings. Some team members may feel some concern about defending ratings in areas with which they feel unfamiliar. This is not a problem. First, during the orientation, reviewers gain competence in making ratings by examining illustrations deserving low and high ratings on each criteria. Illustrations drawn from old applications and masked so the identity of the applicant is not apparent will be especially helpful. Second, all of the criteria represent areas where the ordinary, thoughtful, and interested citizen can make judgments. Third, reviewers are not obligated to defend summary ratings, except extreme ones. The ratings are presented as the collective judgment of a group of reviewers weighing a complex set of factors. In those cases of extreme ratings where defense is called for, one or more team members will be able to present the rationale for the rating. In short, the use of ratings based on criteria is a sound procedure that greatly increases the fairness and comprehensiveness of funding decisions.

CONFLICTS OF INTEREST

While most funding organizations try very hard to see that reviewers who have vested interests in an application do not take part in the funding decision, and indeed most reviewers try not to put themselves in such a position, it occasionally happens. Applicants sometimes think it happens far more often than it does. A written and widely distributed conflict of interest policy reinforces the idea that funding decisions are made fairly. The policy should be discussed when orienting new reviewers and handed out to all reviewers annually. Some organizations prefer reviewers to sign a conflict of interest agreement, while others believe a reminder is sufficient.

A conflict of interest policy should include the provision that reviewers do not make motions or seconds, vote, or speak on behalf of applicants on whose board they sit. Nor do they take these actions when a relative is an employee of the applicant. Reviewers who do business with the applicant should also absent themselves from such actions. A well-publicized conflict of interest policy will add much to the credibility of the funding process.

POWERS OF THE FUNDING ORGANIZATION

There is a fine line between making budgetary adjustments and

DATE: _____ _____ _____

                                    (Mo.)   Day   Year

PROGRAM RATING SUMMARY FORM

Original ☐   Revised ☐

	A Great Deal	Considerably	A Moderate Amount	Very Little	Not At All	Average Of All Ratings
1. To what extent are salary increases and benefits consistent with those requested by similar programs and salary guidelines?	5	4	3	2	1	
2. To what extent are income projections accurate and realistic?	5	4	3	2	1	
3. To what extent are projections of expenses accurate, based on sound information, and fully justified?	5	4	3	2	1	

	Fully	Almost Entirely	Moderate Degree	Violated	Total Disregard	
4. To what extent did program management follow last year's recommendations?	5	4	3	2	1	

	Much Above Av.	Above Av.	Aver- age	Below Av.	Much Below Av.	Average of All Ratings

5. How cost effective has the program been since the last allocation?

	5	4	3	2	1	

6. Overall, how effective is the fiscal planning and management of the program?

	5	4	3	2	1	

7. How successful has the program been in providing services since the last allocation relative to previous years?

	5	4	3	2	1	

	Very High	High	Moder- ate	Low	

8. What is the need for the service provided by the program?

	4	3	2	1	

	Much Above Av.	Above Av.	Aver- age	Below Av.	Much Below Av.	Average Of All Ratings

9. How successful is the program in comparison to other programs of a similar type?

	5	4	3	2	1	

PROFILE OF AVERAGE RATINGS

	Salary	Income Projections	Expense proportions	Conform to Funding Organ. Recom. & Pol.	Cost-Effectiveness	Overall Fiscal Planning & Mgmt.	Effect of Change	Success Since Last Alloc.	Need for Service	Success in Comparison to Similar Programs
Highest 5										
4										
3										
2										
Lowest 1										

Overall Average Rating _____

becoming involved in the internal governance of the agency applying for funds. While some matters over which funding organizations have jurisdiction are governed by law and regulations, others are not. Ordinarily, the funding organization legitimately has the power to (1) regulate how the funds can be spent and the extent to which cross-category transfers of funds can be made, (2) make funding contingent on the outcome of financial or management audits, if review indicates one is needed, (3) make funding contingent on the outcome of a feasibility study, (4) make funding contingent on conformity to funding organization guidelines and regulations, (5) specify that the agency change its financial record keeping practices, (6) make review of the application contingent on a correct and complete application, and (7) make part of the year's funding (e.g., two months) contingent on compliance with funding organization regulations and rules. On the other hand, funding organizations do not ordinarily have the power to make funding contingent on the hiring or firing of certain personnel, change the organizational structure, or alter the methods of serving clients. These are matters for the professional staff and the governing board of the agency.

Even in cases where the review group feels the chief executive is inept, the funding organization should do no more than furnish the evidence that there are management problems and some of the consequences of these problems that have become evident in the course of reviewing the agency's application.

Funding organizations have an opportunity to do some creative work in helping to restore faltering programs. Specifically, funders can create incentives for program executives to improve their program. For example, a funding organization could agree to fund 80 percent of the current year's request, unless the agency increased service levels to a certain point. If the agency meets the new standard, it would be eligible to receive 100 percent of their request. The recommendation needs to be accompanied by offers of technical assistance as well as by specific suggestions as to how service levels can be increased with current resources. Such measures can give the management of an agency a strong incentive to improve the operation.

RECOMMENDATIONS FOR AGENCY EXECUTIVES

Agencies and funding organizations need each other. Both have program obligations to fulfill that require the cooperation of the other. Agency executives need not be hesitant to make suggestions that would improve the funding process. They might make suggestions collectively through representation on funding organization committees or through their own organization of agency executives. Feedback (optimally after each funding cycle) on the funding process is valuable for both parties and brings them into a closer working relationship.

It is to the agency executive's best interest to respond to all of the questions on the application as completely as possible. If the funding organization keeps its forms and procedures up to date, some member of the review group will be interested in each question on the application. By not answering some questions or giving cursory attention to the item, some reviewer is going to respond by giving a lower rating on the criterion for which that information is relevant.

If the applicant is not certain what information is wanted in response to a particular question, ask representatives of the review group. Look at old applications that were successful in previous years. Attend orientation meetings. Talk to other agency executives. Pay close attention to the feedback received on the preceding year's applications. The more information you have about what the reviewers are looking for, the greater the likelihood of being funded.

Chapter 5

EVALUATING HUMAN SERVICE AGENCIES

WHAT IS EVALUATION?

Program evaluation is the process of assessing how well a human service organization is reaching its goals. Goals are statements of intent to bring about a change in the client population's behavior, circumstances, or well-being. "To reduce drug abuse problems among teenagers;" "To reduce malnutrition in Lincoln's noninstitutionalized elderly;" "To increase feelings of self-worth in people experiencing divorce;" these are examples of goals. To achieve such goals, human service agencies operate programs. Programs consist of activities (counseling, providing recreational opportunities, offering classes, making referrals) and resources (staff, volunteers, dollars) arranged to achieve the agencies' goals. Evaluation is the process of gathering information about the agency, weighing it, and coming up with a balanced judgement about the impact the organization is having.

Assessing program impact can be done in many ways. Evaluation can determine whether one mode of treatment is better than another. For example, is individual counseling superior to group work? Evaluation can determine whether preventive recreational and personal development programs actually prevent delinquency or mental illness. Estimating the proportion of human services resources that actually reach the client is still another way of assessing program impact. Assessments such as these would require expensive and complex evaluation studies using sophisticated methods of measurement and analysis. While such studies would provide information valuable for general policy decisions, the data would not be very useful for making funding decisions at the local level.

A more suitable way to assess program impact at the local level is to address the general question: How well is the agency doing what it is supposed to be doing? Evaluation can answer such questions as: Is the agency delivering services efficiently? Are clients satisfied? Is the staff informed and productive? Is agency management effective? What can be done to improve the agency's productivity? All of these questions are matters that can be handled through short-term and inexpensive evaluation studies and provide information valuable in making funding decisions about the agency.

USES OF EVALUATION

While every funding organization does some evaluation in the process of reviewing applications, usually the evaluation focuses on a limited range of issues surrounding the budget and seldom deals with other matters in any detail. Evaluation studies conducted apart from the funding review process can provide a more complete review of the agency's operation, which identifies its major strengths and weaknesses. Information needed to make the types of programmatic ratings called for in the preceding chapter (making funding decisions) is an invaluable product of evaluation. Evaluations serve as a guide to future funding decisions, as they provide a benchmark against which progress and decline can be assessed. The detailed information that comes from evaluations is a strong base from which to make funding decisions. Programs that are going to yield a higher return for the investment are more easily identified, as are those that represent a greater risk when expansion funds are being considered. Evaluations can serve as a basis for developing financial incentives (for example, holding back funds until certain problems are corrected) for an agency to overcome deficiencies in its delivery of services. They provide a sound basis upon which to award additional funds to help overcome a particular problem (for example, to improve record keeping or increase fee collection). Evaluations yield information useful in making decisions to reduce funding for an aspect of an agency's operation that seems to be losing ground over a period of time. Finally, and perhaps more importantly, evaluations can be used to demonstrate accountability to taxpayers, donors, and superiors.

WHAT ARE THE LIMITATIONS OF PROGRAM EVALUATIONS?

While the benefits of a program evaluation are great, there are limitations to what can be achieved. Locally funded and sponsored evaluations must by necessity be limited in both the time it takes to complete them and the human and financial resources that can be allocated to them. While it is possible to conduct thorough and useful evaluations under such constraints, there are some matters that cannot be addressed. It is unlikely, for example, that an evaluation of the scope we are proposing would detect a staff member embezzling funds. A skilled accountant with considerable time would be needed to make such a determination. As noted above, it is not possible to assess complex program outcome or the relative effectiveness of alternative modes of treatment. It is also unlikely such evaluations can resolve a severe management problem or a bitter internal conflict. Evaluators will detect such problems and propose procedures for resolving them, but evaluation cannot see them through a resolution.

WHEN TO EVALUATE AND WHEN NOT TO EVALUATE

There are a number of factors that should be considered in deciding whether or not to evaluate an agency. None of the following guidelines are hard and fast rules. One factor may override another, so that while there are a number of reasons not to conduct an evaluation, the reasons to proceed may be more compelling.

1. An agency that is going through extensive changes is not a good candidate for evaluation. An agency with an impending or recent change in the executive director or other key administrative officers should not be evaluated until the organization has had time (six months or a year) to adjust to the change. Agencies just getting underway or embarking on a major new program should be avoided. The reason for not evaluating during a period of rapid change is that few people will take the report as an accurate

statement of the agency's performance for more than a few months after the study.

2. An agency about which funding organization administrators have very strong views as to the agency's value are also poor prospects for evaluation. The evaluation will not be taken seriously unless it conforms to prevailing views of the agency. There is little point in spending the time and energy necessary to do the study if it is not going to be used.

3. There is little value in evaluating an agency where the executive director is strongly opposed to the study. Executives dragged into an evaluation kicking and screaming will not provide the support and information needed to do an effective job. Much resistance can be overcome by making the benefits of evaluation known to executives. Agency executives that have found evaluations to be helpful and productive should be asked to make presentations. Agency executives who are resistant should be given plenty of opportunity to air their objections. Perhaps some of the objections are justified and indicate ways the evaluation process might be improved upon. There should be no secrets in the evaluation process. Agency executives should know exactly what to expect. Copies of the manual guiding the evaluation process should be sent to agencies on a regular basis. One procedure that will help familiarize the executives with the process and remove some of the we/they feeling sometimes associated with evaluation is to put an executive from an agency not currently being reviewed on each evaluation team.

4. An agency that is suspected of performing marginally should be evaluated. Evaluation presents the opportunity to pinpoint weak spots and offer technical assistance that would help current deficiencies.

5. New programs that have been in operation for two or three years are good candidates. Evaluation can serve to assess the still uncertain costs and benefits to the agency. Moreover, evaluation can identify strengths and weaknesses at a time when the agency is still in its formative stage and is more open to alteration.

WHO SHOULD CONDUCT AGENCY EVALUATIONS?

Funding organizations could hire consulting firms from outside the community to conduct evaluations. While such firms may be unbiased, they are not knowledgeable about the community in which the service is being provided, and they are expensive. Moreover, there is evidence (cf. Van deVall and Belas, 1979) that evaluations done internally are much more likely to be used and accepted. Therefore, evaluations conducted by local people are highly desirable.

On the other hand, none of the people conducting a particular evaluation should be on the staff or board of the agency being evaluated. It is difficult for evaluation team members to be open and candid in their discussions in the presence of an agency representative. Moreover, users of the evaluation will not believe it was conducted impartially if agency insiders were members of the group conducting the evaluation.

The funding organization sponsoring evaluation could hire three or four people with advanced degrees in evaluation and charge them with the responsibility of evaluating twenty agencies per year. However, not only is this option prohibitively expensive, but such a team would quickly be defined as erudite, out of touch, and irrelevant. A far more desirable approach is to assemble teams of people from funding agency staff, volunteer groups such as United Way, human service agency executives, city employees, and county staff. They should be individuals whose primary job is not program evaluation, but people with an interest in human services. The diverse backgrounds of such individuals will ensure thorough evaluations that will be respected by the agency as well as the funding organization and its constituents. By drawing on volunteers and spreading the work over a wide variety of organizations, charges of diverting funds from direct service, which are sometimes directed at planning and evaluation programs, will not be given much credibility.

It is recommended that people be organized into teams of six to eight individuals that would conduct one or two agency evaluations each year. Team composition should be diverse. No team should be composed of all agency executives, city employees, or funding agency staff. The executive director of the agency being evaluated should have the opportunity to say if any of the team members might have a conflict of interest and request a replacement.

While the chair of the team can guide the group through the

evaluation process, there is a need for staff support. An individual should be assigned to each team who can provide information, arrange meetings, handle correspondence, assemble materials, keep records, and arrange for typing and other secretarial services. An employee of the funding organization might be assigned the task. The person should not be a regular voting member of the team.

It is important that the sponsor of evaluations be at an administrative level higher than the agencies being evaluated. If the funding agency is sponsoring the evaluations, this is not a problem. If the funding organization assigns sponsorship of the evaluations to a planning or research group that is at the same level as the agencies being evaluated, the evaluations will not be regarded seriously, and it will be difficult to get cooperation.

ORGANIZING A PROGRAM FOR EVALUATING HUMAN SERVICE AGENCIES ON A REGULAR BASIS

An example of how one community organized a program of regular agency evaluations might be helpful. Through a process described in detail in Chapter Seven, the Lincoln-Lancaster County United Way Planning Division became the planning group for all fifty human service agencies in the area. One of their primary responsibilities is program evaluation.

The Planning Division consists of approximately fifty volunteers. A few are agency executives (representing human service agency executive associations), but most are individuals from a variety of occupational backgrounds (including housewives and retired persons) who have an interest in human services and contributing to the community. Many are members of one or more agency boards and have done other volunteer work. The membership is divided into six teams. Each team is responsible for evaluating two agencies each year. At the beginning of each year, the teams receive four hours of training. The training procedures are described in detail later in this chapter.

The teams are staffed by United Way's Planning Director, a United Way student intern, and the county's Human Services Coordinator. The combined time they devote to evaluation is equivalent to 1.0 full-time equivalent. Staff assignments depend on the funding sources for the agency being evaluated.

The chairs of the six teams comprise the Evaluation Committee, which is responsible for the training of the teams, reviewing and updating the evaluation manual, and scheduling the evaluations. The Evaluation Committee meets on other occasions to discuss particular problems teams are having. The wide variety of experience these team leaders have had means there are few problems that are not readily resolved without outside help.

The paragraphs that follow are the nuts and bolts section of the evaluation manual team members use to guide their evaluation (United Way of Lincoln and Lancaster County, 1983). The introductory paragraphs, omitted here, simply tell how teams are composed, the nature of evaluation, and the limitations of evaluation—materials covered earlier in this chapter. The text is written as if the reader is a new evaluation team member.

A Manual for Evaluation Team Members

Procedures

Before the First Team Meeting

Before your first team meeting, you will receive a packet of information about the agency to be evaluated. The packet will contain promotional material used by the agency, by-laws, articles of incorporation, statement of personnel procedures, most recent budget submissions, financial statements and other materials agency administrators feel you should have to understand their program. A four-year statistical summary compiled by the agency will also be included in the information packet. The summary will include statistics showing the agency's budget, staff, clientele, and use of volunteers.

1. Read or reread the Evaluation Manual so that you are familiar with the task you are about to undertake.
2. Read through the packet of materials before your first team meeting. The familiarity with the program you will gain by reading the material will help you identify aspects of the program's operation that need to be explored during the evaluation. Familiarity with the material will mean shorter meetings and less duplication of effort.
3. While reading through the packet of materials, jot down

questions that come to mind that you want to see covered during the course of the evaluation.

At the First Team Meeting

The purpose of the initial meeting is: (1) to decide on the topics you want to be sure to cover during the evaluation; (2) decide on how you want to collect information; (3) divide the labor among the team members; and (4) draw up a timetable for the project. The tasks that need to be completed at this meeting are:

1. Identify the central components of the program which should be evaluated. The budget may be a guide here— you may decide that each aspect of the program that has a separate budget line is the best definition of a component. It is difficult, however, to evaluate every aspect of a complex human service agency; and sometimes it's hard to reach a consensus on those aspects that should be evaluated.

2. As a result of reading agency materials or something in the news, some team members may have identified questions to which they wish to devote special attention. Make sure all such issues are raised and there is a consensus as to what should be explored.

3. List the types of information that will be needed. (See pages 115-120 of this manual for a list of information that may be valuable.) After each type, list possible sources (administrators, board members, staff, volunteers, clients, agency records, published reports). By this time you should have a good idea of the work to be done.

4. Divide up the work among team members, making sure that *specific* assignments are given to each person. There are no hard and fast rules for this. It depends on the size and organization of the agency being evaluated and on team members' interests. You may decide to make different team members responsible for different program components; types of information; sources of information (clients, staff, board members, volunteers, records); topics to be covered in the final report; or some combination of these. Also decide who is going to be responsible for putting it all together.

5.   An evaluation timetable should be derived as follows:
      Decide on the date you want to have the report
      reviewed by the organization sponsoring the evaluation.
      Leave seven days for support staff to type and distribute
      the report before the meeting. Allow three to four
      weeks before final typing for review by the board of the
      agency being evaluated. At least a week will be needed
      for members of the evaluation team to review and
      rewrite a draft of the report. Allow two to three weeks
      for collecting and assessing information.
6.   The chair should obtain all members' free time in
      succeeding weeks so that he/she can schedule meetings.

Collecting Information

1.   At the first team meeting, team members should prepare
      questions they wish to ask at the agency site visit(s).
      These questions should be sent to the agency adminis-
      trator prior to the first site visit. The agency administrator
      should be encouraged to put replies in writing. This will
      help make the site visits less time consuming and more
      productive.
2.   The chair of the team should arrange meetings with
      agency personnel. Meetings with administrators should
      be scheduled first and should be attended by the entire
      team. This gives administrators a chance to learn about
      the scope and nature of the team's activities. In addition,
      the administrator can smooth the way for subsequent
      data gathering.
3.   The agency director may prefer that the team schedule a
      separate meeting with board members so as not to deal
      with board matters during the initial meeting with
      administrators.
4.   Separate meetings should be scheduled with staff,
      clients and volunteers. Staff should not be present when
      talking to clients so that clients feel free to engage in full
      and open discussion. Whenever possible, schedule
      meetings one right after another on the same day. This
      makes efficient use of team member time and in many
      cases will minimize disruption of the agency's day-to-
      day operation. During the site visits, all interviews with

agency staff, volunteers and clients should be attended by *at least* two team members. In no case should team members conduct interviews individually. This reduces pressure on team members and ensures a more thorough exploration of pertinent questions.

5.   Encourage the administrator to select staff, clients, volunteers and board members to meet with the team members. Ask him or her to select people with diverse views and from different aspects of the program. While this may appear to be stacking the deck in the agency's favor, it seldom, if ever, results in significant information not reaching the evaluation team. By talking to a variety of people and asking good questions, the team can get information on all aspects of the program.

6.   The number of clients, staff, volunteers and board members the team talks to should be large enough to gather a diversity of information but small enough so that neither the team nor the agency resources are taxed. Depending on the size of the agency, the team should try to talk to at least six clients and six staff members. If volunteers are not a significant part of the agency's operation, the team may choose not to talk to any volunteers. Board members may also be omitted if sufficient information is obtained about their activities from the administrator and published documents.

7.   After obtaining information about the reports and documents that might provide information useful in the evaluation, make arrangements to obtain these from the agency or other sources. The material may be of such a nature (bulky or confidential) that it cannot be removed from the agency's office. Team members should make arrangements to visit the site to review the information. The team may be able to copy other materials that can be assimilated later.

8.   Team members should contact other organizations with which the agency has cooperative working relationships to discuss their assessments of the agency. Obtain contact names from the agency administrator.

9.   Team support staff can be of help in scheduling meet-

ings and obtaining documents and other materials that could be of use in the evaluation. The assigned staff member will also sit in on all team meetings, assist in keeping records, and serve as a source of information on the agency's relation to funding sources and other matters. While staff members are not voting members of the evaluation team, they are active participants.

10.　Some team members may wish to hold a wind-up meeting with agency administrators to cover loose ends or to cover material missed during the data collection phase.

Reviewing and Assessing Information

Once agency site visits are completed, a team meeting should be scheduled for the team to review the information gathered and attempt to formulate judgments and make recommendations pertaining to those judgments. This should be scheduled immediately after the site visits are concluded so that the information does not go stale (and it goes stale fast). Members may discover that certain vital information is still missing. Usually this can be obtained with a phone call or two. If consensus is not reached on all matters, a third meeting may need to be scheduled. Experience shows that, without the post visit meeting, the report preparation takes more time, more drafts are necessary and team consensus is more difficult to obtain.

Each aspect of the agency's report should be discussed at the meeting. As each topic is considered, see if consensus can be reached. Once consensus is achieved, review possible recommendations that would help to overcome program deficiencies.

Once all major topics have been covered, the content of the report should be clear. Decide on major headings if the format is to be different than the one recommended at the end of this manual. Agree on a schedule for the preparation of the final report: draft, team review, and transmission to the agency.

Report Preparation

Once a draft of the report is completed, support staff will type, copy and send copies of it to team members. Minor editing, organization and wording changes can be handled by phone. If one or more team members seriously objects to a section of the report, a team meeting should be called to resolve the difference or to plan a minority report.

Agency and Funding Organization Approval

Once the entire team approves the report, it is ready for review by the agency which has been evaluated. Staff will submit a clean copy to the agency for its review.

Team members should keep in mind that, in addition to being one of the primary consumers of the evaluation, agency staff have more than a passing interest in the contents of the study. While they may be gratified by the appreciation shown for the strengths of the program, they may be upset about one or more of the weaknesses identified. If the evaluation team has been conscientious in its task, however, there should be no surprises. During the course of the meetings with agency staff, team members should have discussed problems they encountered to get some idea of the way in which agency staff are trying to deal with them.

Occasionally team recommendations for shoring up problem areas may be unclear or impractical due to some aspect of the situation about which team members were unaware. In cases where the agency staff feel the report is unfair, inaccurate or impractical, the team should arrange a meeting to discuss the issues. On the basis of new information or re-analysis, the team may choose to revise some of its findings and recommendations to make the report a more useful document. In other cases, they may feel there is insufficient new information to alter the report. In this instance they must convince the agency staff and board of directors that the report is a fair assessment, as agency board acknowledgement is required for the report to be forwarded to the funding organization sponsoring the evaluation. The agency may prepare a written rebuttal which then becomes part of the team report. The agency is not to publicize the report until it has been approved by the funding organization.

Prior to the meeting at which the funding organization considers the report, copies are distributed to members. At the meeting, the chair of the team makes a brief report and moves the adoption of the report. After discussion, and sometimes amendments, the report is approved. It is then sent to the agency under review and any other appropriate organizations. Six months following approval, funding organization staff will meet with agency administrators to review the organization's progress in meeting the recommendations.

What Do You Want To Find Out?

Goals

The first thing team members must fully understand are the goals of the program. All else follows from a thorough grasp of the goals. The goals are the criteria against which progress is measured and form the basis upon which comparisons can be made with other programs.

Goals should clearly identify the target population which the program is trying to assist, such as elderly homeowners or people with drug abuse problems. Goals should clearly state the change which is expected to occur as a result of being a client in the program. The identity of the target population and the desired change should be stated in clear, operational terms. That means terms that most people would agree on if they saw them. A good way to think about a goal is to ask yourself the question: Is it something that can be measured? "To enhance psycho-social development" is not a clear operational statement. No mention of a target population is given, and the meaning of psycho-social is vague. "To increase feelings of independence among elderly persons who are disabled" is measurable. You can count the number of things elderly people can do for themselves, or you can ask them if they feel more independent as a result of their participation in the program.

Goals are often stated in ambiguous terms—partly because they come from technical jargon; partly to please legislators who find it easier to vote for a bill if it is stated in general terms; and partly because no one has bothered to take the time to develop a clear set of goals. When faced with a set of unclear goals, team members should try to translate them into operational terms with the help of program administrators. A thorough discussion of the matter will usually result in a set of goals that evaluators and program personnel agree on.

Sources. Printed material promoting the agency, budget applications. Goal clarification is obtained in discussions with agency administrators.

Need for the Program

A two-fold purpose is served in obtaining information on the need for the program. The first is to evaluate the extent to which the program is serving a need not met by other human service organizations. The second is to see whether or not the agency's staff is well informed about the size and nature of their target population and changes in the target population which may be occurring in the near future.

Over the next few years, there will be an ever-pressing need to use the available human service dollars more efficiently. Therefore, it is important to gather information on the extent to which the agency has a target population and services which are unique from those of other human service agencies. Detailed information on the characteristics (age, sex, residence and condition) of the target population and the number being reached should be gleaned about the agency being evaluated and about other local agencies with similar or related goals. The proportion of the target population being reached is important in identifying unmet needs.

Determining exactly what services are provided by the agency is also crucial in order to gain a clear idea of the extent to which efforts are being duplicated. A key question to ask yourself (as well as agency administrators) is: "What would happen if the agency ceased to exist?" Information on other agencies that have a similar target population (but different service) or similar service (but different target population) may suggest possible avenues of consolidation in the event scarce resources make such a strategy necessary.

A sign of quality in an organization is how much administrators know about their target populations. Administrators should be knowledgeable about census data, input from client groups and studies that document the current size of the target population and whether or not it will undergo changes in the near future which would have a bearing on the demand for the agency's services. In short, administrators should be able to document the need for the program in no uncertain terms. Poor information on the need for the program could indicate an uninformed administrator, an unwillingness to acknowledge unfavorable trends or other problems that should be explored by the evaluation team.

Sources. Current funding applications, promotional materials. Administrators may be able to provide reports of pertinent studies from their professional associations or journals. Evaluations of the agency conducted by other organizations may be a source of such information.

Program Strengths and Weaknesses

To understand most of the larger human service programs, the evaluation team needs to break these down into components and examine them separately. Budget program categories are a good place to start. In cases where an array of services are offered in a single budgeted program, a more detailed breakdown may be necessary. Once the separate components are identified, team members should become acquainted with what happens to the clients as they proceed through the program. Who do clients talk to and how often? In what activities do clients engage? What does the client experience at the beginning, middle and end of participation in the program?

A grasp of the resources (staff, facilities and equipment, activities or service units) the agency brings to bear on each client is also essential. With respect to staff, one should determine the professional staff-to-client ratio and the administrator-to-staff ratio. These figures allow one to compare the agency with similar programs or some standard to see whether the agency being evaluated is making more or less efficient use of personnel. Other questions to explore include: How much formal training do staff members have? How much in-service training do staff members receive? How much experience does the professional staff have?

With respect to material resources, obtain information on the amount allocated to each client. Material costs per client is a general figure that may be a useful guide. But it may also be desirable to gather information with respect to specific materials, such as books, pamphlets and other disposable resources. Facilities may be defined in terms of space or room per client. Equipment may be viewed in terms of clients per piece of equipment. Each area of human service will have its own way of defining the availability of material resources. Team members should learn about them and use them in their evaluation. The amount spent per service unit delivered is another general point of reference that is basic to understanding the quality of the services delivered.

Finally, team members should learn how success is defined. Every program should have a clear and precise definition of what constitutes a successful client. The proportion (percent) of clients who are successful should be obtained and compared with that of other programs or some standard.

All recent changes should be explored in detail since they also indicate problems or achievements. Large staff turnover can indicate a problem. Increasing number of clients or staff may indicate a new approach. Decline in the number of clients may reveal that another agency is serving the same population. Such changes are fruitful areas of inquiry.

The key to evaluation is comparison of the agency's current program and achievements with: A set of generally accepted standards; those of agencies with similar target populations and services; and with the agency's own past performance. Ideally, teams would be able to make comparisons in all three areas. Frequently, data is unavailable or incomplete, and teams must make do with what is available.* By comparing the program (staff, consumable and fixed resources, cost per service unit, etc.) and the extent to which the agency is achieving its goals (percent of clients who are successful) with standards, other programs, or past performance, the team can obtain some measure of how well the agency is doing. It is important that comparisons be made with standards for similar sized agencies and that the agency only be compared with one of a similar character. The selection of similar agencies must be done with care.

Sources. Interviews with staff, volunteers and clients are excellent sources of information. Reports and documents provided by administrators are another. A tour of the facilities and observations of staff and clients in action are other valuable sources, although they are time-consuming for the amount of information they yield.

Financial Outlook

To gain perspective on the agency's current and future

---

*In cases where information is poor, evaluation teams may want to recommend securing better information for future evaluations.

financial outlook, it is advisable for team members to examine income and expenditures over the last three to five years. Decreases in funds may be the source of problems. Increases may cue team members to growth difficulties. Increases in income from fees or new sources of funds may indicate planning and effort in anticipation of a decline in tax support. Team members should inquire into the stability of existing sources to see whether declines are indicated and, if so, the extent to which the agency is planning for these declines. Can fees be raised without cutting off significant segments of the target population? Can insurance or other third-party payments be tapped for some of the services rendered? Are grants being sought from local, state and federal sources? If program expansion is planned, are the financial resources adequate to cope with the expansion without jeopardizing other aspects of the program? These are among the questions that should be examined in order to evaluate the financial outlook of the agency.

Sources. Recent budget applications are most revealing. These documents also contain information on expenses. Other details may be obtained from administrators.

Evaluation and Planning

Every agency should regularly evaluate its program as a basis for achieving greater efficiency, setting priorities and planning. Ideally, the agency should be involved in long-term as well as short-term evaluations. These evaluations should involve the systematic collection of information about the organization from a variety of sources (clients, staff, etc.) as well as comparative data from external sources. A variety of techniques should be used to evaluate the data to insure an impartial evaluation. Review by ad hoc committees consisting of board members, administrators and staff is one technique that minimizes bias. Review by outsiders is another. Also, there should be a mechanism for incorporating the results of the evaluation back into the programs. The material contained in this manual may help the team to assess the agency's evaluation program.

Planning is another activity that should be a regular part of every agency's operation and goes hand in hand with the evaluation process. There should be evidence that information on new approaches, emerging needs of the target population, and changes in the target population is gathered and reviewed regularly. It should be used as a basis for setting priorities and guiding program operation and development for extended periods (three to five years) and shorter periods (one to three years).

Sources. The primary source of information on evaluation and planning activities will be administrators. Board members may be valuable informants as well. Any reports stemming from evaluation and planning activities should also be examined.

Internal Management Procedures

There are a variety of widely accepted and sound management practices for human service agencies that team members should review. Many represent regulations by funding agencies. Most will be self-evident as team members review the materials provided by the agency and talk to staff and clients. Therefore, they are presented here as a simple check list for which one team member can assume responsibility during the course of the evaluation.

Sources. Some of this information will be contained in materials you receive before the evaluation. Some will become apparent as you proceed through the evaluation. The remainder can be obtained by interview with the agency administrator.

Gathering Information

In the course of gathering information from the various sources, keep notes on important points as you go along. Don't rely on the support staff or others to carry out this function as they may regard the information you think is central as only a matter of passing interest. Each member of the evaluation team brings a different perspective to the task. It is this variation in points of view that makes it possible to arrive at a broad-gauged and fair evaluation. By keeping your own notes, you are assured that your own perspective is going to be fully reflected in the final report.

In addition to recording information, record questions that come to mind that you want to have addressed later. This, too, insures a comprehensive exploration of the agency being evaluated. Record the exact phrasing of the information you obtain. This helps you become familiar with the unique wording agency staff may use in describing their activities. Also, it is valuable in preparing a final report. Correct phrasing indicates the team has a clear understanding of the agency's mission and operation.

It is often advantageous to begin collecting information of a general nature by inquiring about problems that clients, staff, volunteers and administrators experience in the delivery of services. Information on the most valuable aspects of the program may also be gathered by general questioning. Beginning with general information, get at those things most on the minds of agency staff and clients; and identify elements of the program that should explored in detail. Such questioning goes a long way toward setting the agenda for the evaluation.

Notes on Interviewing

Interviewing clients, staff, volunteers and administrators is perhaps the richest source of information in an evaluation. As such, it is important to use this resource with care and efficiency. The wrong approach can greatly diminish the value of the interview as an information-gathering device. Often agency staff and clients are apprehensive about evaluation. Few people cherish the idea of "outsiders peering over their shoulder to see how good a job they are doing." The following suggestions will minimize the chance of losing this resource:

1.　At the outset of each interview, introduce all team members and who they represent. Learn the names of people being interviewed. It is a friendly gesture.
2.　Explain that the funding organization sponsoring the study has the task of evaluating all human service programs every few years and that the meeting is part of that process.
3.　Indicate that the purpose of the evaluation is to obtain information that would make the agency an even better organization than it is. Stress the positive.
4.　When talking to staff, clients and volunteers, indicate that anything they say will be held in confidence and that the identity of the person who said it will not be revealed to the administrator. When appropriate, indicate to the clients that their identity is a confidential matter and that it will not be revealed to anyone outside the interview.

Asking Questions

1. Ask direct questions. Don't beat around the bush or ask vague or indirect questions. Interviewees appreciate a direct approach. It encourages direct answers.
2. Remain neutral throughout the course of the interview. Even if you feel that what the interviewee is saying is grossly wrong or she/he is making bigoted or unpleasant statements, do not reveal your own opinion on the matter. To do so will merely influence the rest of what the respondent says and thus limit the quality of the information you obtain.
3. Don't preach. If you wish to get the interviewee's attitude on some matter, ask: "How do you feel about . . .?
4. Keep the convesation natural rather than rigidly following a set of questions. Many of the items team members wish to explore will come up in the course of conversation. Ask about them as they arise.

The following are questions you may find useful when interviewing people in the program.

Administrators

-What are the strongest (most effective) parts of your program?

-What parts of your program are weakest (in most need of improvement)?

-What do you see as the chief problems facing the program? or

-What aspects of the program would you like to see changed?

-How do you measure success?

-What is the current success rate?

-How does your success rate compare with similar agencies?

-Have there been recent changes in your success rate?

-Why aren't you successful with some people? Is that something you can do anything about?

-What sort of people should you be reaching but are having trouble doing so?

-What makes them difficult to reach? Do you have plans to solve this problem?

-If you were facing a 20 percent decrease in funds next year, what would you cut?

Clients
   -How did you come to be a part of the program?
   -Is the program helping you? How?
   -Is there anything you would like to see changed? or
   -Is there something the staff could do so that you would get
   more out of the program?
   -Do you feel like your ideas are taken into account by the
   staff?
   -What are the most valuable aspects of the program?

Professional Staff
   -Tell me about your background: formal training, experience
   in similar programs, and how long you have been in this
   program.
   -What do you do in a typical day?
   -How would you rate this program relative to similar pro-
   grams you know about?
   -What aspects of the program are most effective?
   -What parts of the program need to be improved?
   -Do you feel that you should get more recognition than you
   do for your contribution to the program?

Board Members
   -How much impact do you have on the program?
   -Do you feel that you are kept well informed about the
   program's problems and prospects?
   -What are the major problems facing the program as you see
   it?
   -What aspects of the program would you like to see changed?
   -If funds were reduced by 20 percent, what aspects of the
   program would you select for cutting?

Volunteers
   -How did you come to be a volunteer?
   -Do you feel that you received enough training to do a
   competent job?
   -Do you feel that you are being used as effectively as you
   could be? or
   -Do you feel underutilized?
   -Do you receive sufficient recognition for what you do?
   -What could be changed to make the program more effec-
   tive?
   -What are the program's strong points?

Arriving at Balanced Judgements

Coming up with a fair judgment about the effectiveness with which a program is reaching its goals is not an easy task. Few programs are exceptionally effective, and most have a number of areas that could stand to be improved. And, it's important to bear in mind that even the worst program has a strong point or two that should be reinforced.

Everyone on the team will have opinions about the effectiveness of the program so that generating judgments is not difficult. The key to coming up with balanced judgments is evidence—something which may be more difficult to find. A judgment backed by concrete illustrations, studies or other information will be more fair than one which is not.

For each program or part of a program, the chair should solicit judgments from team members. Once an evaluation is on the floor, team members should offer evidence supporting and contrary to the judgment. Once the evidence is in, the chair should assess team consensus on the judgment by taking votes. Whenever possible, evaluations should be based on a clear majority of votes, not on a difference of just one or two votes. Compromise is an essential element in arriving at balanced judgments. And compromise is not as uncommon as the above discussion would suggest. Most team decisions are unanimous. If, however, there is considerable disagreement, parliamentary procedures should be followed so that everyone on the team has the opportunity to participate fully in the discussion.

Judgments

Judgments not favorable to the agency should always be followed by recommendations that would lead to improvement. Evaluation teams have an obligation to offer solutions to solve problems. Because of their familiarity with all aspects of the agency, the team members are in a good position to offer suggestions that might alleviate or at least reduce the problem. The solutions should be specific—suggest concrete steps that would have a direct bearing on improving the situation. Vague solutions are of little value. The solutions should also be practical, that is, not requiring large infusions of new money or firing most of the staff. They should be steps that can be taken in the near future. In fact, a specific timetable might be part of the recommendation. On the other hand, because most team members are not familiar with the day-to-day operation of the agency, recommendations may not be exactly on the mark. During the course of the review by the agency, or even before, recommendations that are more suitable may be derived. These should become part of the report.

Preparing the Report

The evaluation team's report should contain a brief description of the agency in addition to an evaluation. Turnover in some funding groups is high, and the description serves as a valuable anchor point which acquaints new comers with the central features of the organization. The report should be approximately five single-spaced typewritten pages. Brief reports are much more likely to be read. In the pages that follow, an outline of an evaluation team report is proposed. A brief description of material that should be included under each heading is indicated. The categories may not be suitable for all agencies and should be altered to meet special needs.

Name of Agency

Evaluation Team Members
List alphabetically with affiliations of
special representatives

Staff
List alphabetically

Date

Approved by _____ Date_____
(Agency)

Approved by (Funding Organization)   Date _____

Program Description

Overview

In a sentence or two (without any evaluation or comment) describe:

   Recent history of the agency;

   The program—what staff does to achieve the desired change;

   Clients—age, sex, minority status, how they get into the program (referral, walk-in, etc.), and other pertinent characteristics;

   Staff—training, stage in career, experience; and

   Financing—where the money to operate the agency comes from.

Four-Year Statistical Summary

	1981	1982	1983	Current Year Budget
Expenses				
Deficit/Surplus				
Volunteers				
Staff (Full-time equivalent)				
Administration				
Professional				
Other				
Clients by Program Categories				

Evaluation of Program

Need for Program

Describe who the target population is and whether their numbers are increasing or decreasing. Indicate the source of this information. Also, indicate how the agency is different and how it is similar to others and what would happen if the agency ceased to exist. List the priorities established by relevant community funding agencies which the agency's program addresses.

Program Goals

The central goals of the agency should be listed in clear, jargon-free terms. As indicated on page 115 of this manual, they should be stated in measurable terms and focus on change in the client rather than internal administrative matters.

Program Strengths

Pick two to four factors that contribute most importantly to the agency's goals. Do not list everything that is satisfactory. The reader will assume that things which are not mentioned are satisfactory. For each strength, report the team's judgment and describe in some detail the supporting evidence. Conclude with a recommendation where appropriate: for example, encouraging the agency to concentrate more resources in strongest areas, advertise such areas, etc.

Program Weaknesses

Select factors that detract most from the agency achieving its goals. Present judgments and evidence as described above. The recommendations for reducing these weaknesses should follow the discussion of each weakness. The background of the recommendation (why it should diminish the weakness) should be stated as well.

Financial Outlook

Current funding problems should be described. In addition, the team's assessment of the agency's plan to cope with shrinking resources should be stated. Conclude with recommendations where deficiencies are revealed.

Evaluation and Planning

Briefly describe the agency's evaluation and planning activities and report the team's evaluation of these efforts. Recommendations may be included.

Internal Management Practices

Summarize the team's assessment of the management of the agency. Details only need be provided in areas where there are deficiencies. Conclude with recommendations when appropriate.

Summary of Recommendations

Before listing the recommendations in one-sentence statements, provide a brief introduction especially designed for the person who skims the report or reads no other section.

A TRAINING PROGRAM FOR EVALUATION

From the evaluation manual excerpt presented previously, it is evident that the task is complex. Some inexperienced people may not feel qualified to do the work. To help prepare people who are not professionals in the field of evaluation, some training should be conducted. A training program found to be effective is described below. It takes approximately four hours to complete and it can be conducted by a nonprofessional who has chaired at least one evaluation team. Team members are instructed to read their manual before attending the training meeting. At the training meeting, the participants work on four evaluation field problems covering some of the more troublesome aspects of evaluation. All of the field problems involve the evaluation of a fictitious agency called Growing Up Gracefully, or "GUG" as it has become affectionately labeled. The program description below is given to the trainees.

The Growing Up Gracefully Program (GUG) has been providing counseling services to youth between the ages of 10 and 20 since 1968. A grant from the Office of Economic Opportunity got the agency off the ground. Initially designed to serve the economically disadvantaged, it now provides counseling to youngsters from all income levels. Families are charged for services according to their ability to pay. The program is funded by United Way, Joint Budget Committee, and by grants from the Federal Government. Last year the Federal Government cut their grant by 25 percent. As a result, pay raises were forfeited and one open secretarial position was left vacant.

The program is designed to ease the transition from one stage of adolescence to the next through individual and group counseling. Clients are referred by schools, ministers, physicians, and County Welfare, as well as other youth serving agencies. A staff of 15 people provides services with an annual budget of $250,000 to help more than 950 young people a year.

Each problem is considered at the same time by all of the trainees. If there is more than one evaluation team, it is best to have the teams work as a group. This gives the team some experience working together before actually doing an evaluation.

The *first* field problem deals with assessing information provided to the team by the agency before the site visit. In this problem, the following information is presented by the agency to the evaluation team.

GROWING UP GRACEFULLY PROGRAM
Four Year Statistical Summary

	1981	1982	1983	Current Year
Expenses	$211,800	$231,000	$250,000	$225,000
Deficit/Surplus	($2,000)	($3,000)	($3,500)	
Staff (Full-Time Equivalent)				
Administrative	1.25	1.75	2.0	2.0
Professional	10.25	10.75	10.5	10.5
Support	2.5	2.5	2.5	1.5
Volunteers	3	2	2	2
Clients	983	925	866	950 (est.)
Counseling/Interviews				
Individual	2,133	2,104	2,100	2,200 (est.)
Group	98	96	98	100 (est.)

On the basis of this information, the teams are to formulate questions they would ask of the agency director and staff about their operation. The teams are given ten minutes to come up with questions. The person leading the training session calls on each team to present one of their questions. They go from team to team until all the questions have been presented. The training leader should put these on a chalkboard or overhead projector so that team leaders can take notes for future reference and get some idea of the range of information that can be gleaned from agency data. Teams should raise most of the following questions.

1. Why is the deficit climbing?
2. Do you expect the deficit to be more or less in 1984? Why?
3. Why is administrative staff growing in face of declining client population?
4. How are you handling the drop in support staff? Who is doing work for this person?
5. How did you absorb a cut of $25,000 with cutting one low paid support person?
6. Is this a permanent reduction?
7. What is the potential for building up volunteers to handle work suffering from federal cuts?
8. Why is number of clients dropping?
9. Why do you estimate an increase in 1984? On what are they basing the estimate?
10. How do you account for the number of interviews remaining constant while the number of clients is decreasing?
11. Why do you project an increase in the number of interviews in 1984?
12. Why has group work remained constant in face of declining number of clients?

The *second* field problem focuses on situations sometimes encountered in interviewing an agency executive. To give the teams more to work with than the simple descriptions below, have experienced team leaders role play the situations. They should role play in a way that demonstrates poor or inappropriate techniques. After each role play, have the teams answer the question following the situation description.

1. The administration refuses to allow the team to interview clients on the grounds it is an invasion of privacy.

   What arguments or approaches would you use to get access to clients?

2. The administrator talks all around a question about declining client population, but does not give specific information on causes of the decline or what he/she plans to do about it.

What would you do to get around the evasion during the interview?

3. A staff member reveals a personnel turnover problem not mentioned by the administrator.

   How do you tactfully, but thoroughly, explore the problem with the agency executive?

4. Several, but not all, clients report that a particular senior staff member is not attentive to client needs—does not seem to recall previous meetings with the client, appears to doze during interviews, keeps clients waiting for up to thirty minutes without explanation, etc.

   How do you tactfully, but thoroughly, explore the problem with the agency director?

After the teams have had five minutes to work out a solution, the leader of the training group should call on the teams to present solutions. Proceed from team to team until all solutions have been presented. Switch the order in which the teams are called on so that different teams have an opportunity to present their best ideas. The solutions should be put on a chalkboard or overhead projector and the group as a whole asked to select the best one and justify their choice.

The *third* field problem centers on the activities of the team following the site visit where the group is evaluating evidence and coming up with balanced judgements that are then translated into recommendations. Three problems requiring special handling have been devised. After reading the problem, the teams are asked to answer the question following each situation.

1. An active member of the team is reluctant to say anything bad about the agency or its director. The rest of the team is in agreement that the administrator needs to make some adjustments, but the dissenter is adamant. The dissenter objects on grounds that the administrator is a senior agency executive, a nice guy, been in office a long time, has the support of the Board, and that he/she hasn't done that bad of a job.

   What is the most effective way to deal with the dissenter?

2. The team comes to consensus that an agency administrator

who has been in office several years is not doing a good job. Admonishments by the funding organization have been ignored. There is no evidence that funds are being administered effectively. There is no record of the number of clients that have participated in various programs or that various activities sponsored by the organization have even taken place.

Does the evaluation team have the right (or obligation) to recommend that the chief administrator be replaced?

3. The team finds that the agency is very lax about assessing and collecting fees from clients. The funding organization recommended they change their procedures, but the agency has ignored the recommendation.

Should the team recommend that the funding organization cut the agency's appropriation by estimated loss in revenue created by the poor practices?

After giving the teams a few minutes to devise a solution, call upon the groups to present their answer as before. In cases where several viable approaches seem to emerge, the entire group should be encouraged to select the most promising one.

The *fourth* problem has to do with preparing the report. In this case, excerpts from the report on GUG are presented. The last sentence in each paragraph consists of a recommendation with one or more flaws. Assign each team a different paragraph from the following list, and ask them to find the flaw.

1. The agency is open from 9 to 5 on weekdays. Studies show that many students hold part-time jobs in the afternoon and therefore could not use the services without sacrificing needed income and job stability. Therefore, it is recommended that GUG expand hours of operation to include evenings and Saturdays to accommodate working students.

Flaw: Way to expand hours of operation on reduced budget should be addressed.

2. The evaluation team observed that the brochures advertising the program were dated and that there was no plan for getting them into the hands of referral agencies each year. Also, efforts to meet with school counselors to describe the

program and what it can do are limited. As there has been a slight decline in the number of clients served over the last four years, it is recommended that you recruit a volunteer to organize and coordinate a public information program.

Flaw: Not appropriate to ask inexperienced volunteer to take on administrative responsibilities.

3. With the decline in revenues from the Federal Government and a reduction in fee income associated with the decline in clients, GUG is facing financial difficulty for the coming year. It is recommended that GUG seek alternative sources of funds.

Flaw: Should give specific suggestions as to where agency should seek funds.

4. Given the financial emergency, additional efforts should be made to collect delinquent accounts. Therefore, the team recommends that: A secretary be assigned to call all overdue accounts and urge them to pay. Those that do not pay within one month should be assigned to a collection agency.

Flaw: Asking smaller support staff to do more work.

5. The team notes there has been some turnover in the counseling staff in recent years. Five of the ten counselors indicated some dissatisfaction with their salary, pointing out that comparable agencies in other cities were paying their counselors $1,000 more. The team recommends that counselor salaries be raised to a level similar to other teenage counseling services.

Flaw: Asking to spend more money with fewer funds.

6. Little evidence of long-term planning could be identified by the team. Given the declining number of clients and the uncertain funding situation, the team recommends that GUG formulate a ten-year plan for the agency specifying projected needs for services as well as how their needs can be more efficiently met.

Flaw: Ten-year plans in unstable times are an exercise in futility.

7. The GUG board meets six times a year. While the agency director frequently talks with the officers, board members are not actively involved in the agency. Therefore, the team recommends that efforts be made to increase participation of the board in the affairs of the agency.

Flaw: No evidence low board involvement bad, and no suggestions as to how involvement might be altered.

After giving them a few minutes to identify the flaw, the training group leader should summarize the paragraph and ask the appropriate team to describe the flaw. If there aren't enough teams to cover all of the paragraphs, go through the remaining problems with the entire group.

RECOMMENDATIONS FOR AGENCY EXECUTIVES

While funding organizations find evaluations very useful in reaching decisions, the other primary beneficiary is the human service agency being evaluated. It is an opportunity for agency management, staff, and volunteers to take a look at their organization from an outsider's point of view. Buried in the day-to-day operations, problems may go unnoticed, staff may lose sight of the agency's role in the larger community, or the agency may run out of ways to solve a recurring problem. Evaluation can help rectify these matters as well as draw attention to program achievements.

Specifically, program evaluation can be the basis for planning decisions. Objectives can be formulated around dealing with weaknesses and enhancing strengths. Internal resource allocation and the organization of activities can be guided by evaluation results. Agency executives, like funding administrators, can use evaluation as a benchmark against which to measure progress or to document need for financial support. Evaluation results can serve as an integral part of fund applications to document both need and performance.

Chapter 6

ASSESSING HUMAN SERVICE NEEDS

INTRODUCTION

Every funding organization looks for ways to simplify the process of allocating scarce resources without being arbitrary. Sooner or later, someone suggests establishing priorities on the basis of need, and there is general agreement that it seems like a good idea. Developing a set of priorities that enjoy wide acceptance and general use requires care and considerable effort. Therefore, the process should not be entered into lightly.

Assigning priorities to human service needs is a difficult and complex task. A priority assignment system should (1) apply criteria that are widely accepted, (2) draw heavily on high quality information, (3) rely on the judgment of people representing diverse views but who are knowledgeable about and sensitive to human service needs, and (4) recognize the complexity in defining human service needs. The closer any system comes to achieving those goals, the more credibility and use the system will enjoy.

In the paragraphs that follow, the authors describe the way needs were assessed in the City of Lincoln and in Lancaster County. The project took two years to complete and involved the combined efforts of numerous volunteers, agency executives, public officials, and United Way staff. The set of needs and the priorities assigned to them have been used in funding decisions made in 1982 and 1983. There is a plan to reassess needs on a regular basis (every two to three years) to reflect changes in the community and alteration in federal and state funding.

While a well developed set of priorities can be invaluable in reaching fair and informed funding decisions, priorities have important limitations and can be abused. Funding decisions cannot be based solely on priorities. As indicated in Chapter 4, need is only one criteria for funding, and other factors such as the effectiveness of the agency, its efficiency, whether the program is mandated by law, and the strength of the proposal, are among the other equally important factors that need to be considered.

Moreover, priorities are easily abused. If too much weight is given to them, agencies will be encouraged to modify their programs to get them into a higher priority level. A half dozen agencies making major changes in their programs not only creates a good deal of turmoil, but it draws services away from other needy people (adding significantly to the number whose needs are not being met), which could create a serious imbalance in the provision of basic human services in the community.

A more frequent abuse is underutilization of the priorities. Interest in maintaining the status quo, the power of those who support a particular program, and the skill of agency staff in presenting a strong case detract from the use of need assessment studies. This is not all bad. In the final analysis, allocating resources is a question of values, and those values express themselves through complex processes that govern every community. While the needs assessment process described takes into account community values in some ways, it neglects others. It is within the larger political apparatus that the community decides whether it is better to treat adolescent drug abusers or to serve low-income elderly who need in-home services to remain independent. Establishing priorities is but one component of the process.

ORGANIZATION OF A NEEDS ASSESSMENT COMMITTEE

The organization responsible for the needs assessment process described here was the Needs Assessment Committee, a group of sixteen people, half of whom were human service agency executives and the other half volunteers who were members of United Way's Planning Division. It was felt that heavy agency representation was essential to the integrity of the process. The Human Services Federation (the local association of human service agency executives) selected the representatives to participate in the committee.

The work of the Needs Assessment Committee began with devising a list of human service needs that was then refined by drawing on the views of a larger group of agency executives, elected officials, and United Way volunteers. Refining the needs entailed linking the needs to specific programs and getting agency executive agreement on the matter.

The information gathering work of the Needs Assessment Committee was carried on by two subcommittees, the chairs (but not the membership) of which served on the main committee. This served to spread the work around and involve a larger number of people in the overall process. An attitude assessment subcommittee was assigned the task of obtaining information on the need for human services and public attitudes toward providing them from the community at large. A data subcommittee was charged with obtaining estimates of need from human service agency staff.

Once these subcommittees finished their work, the Needs Assessment Committee, based on a review of that information and much discussion, assigned priorities to needs in a four tier system. A set of recommendations was developed on the use of the priorities to help prevent misuse. After one year of use, the priority setting procedure and the utilization of the priorities was evaluated. This was the basis of a decision to go ahead and refine the procedure and continue to use it in future years.

The procedures developed in Lincoln and Lancaster County worked well, and the final product, while not used as fully as it might be, is used extensively. In the paragraphs that follow, the needs assessment process is described in enough detail so that other communities can adapt them for their own use. The reasoning behind various decisions that were made along the way is presented so that the reader can gain some understanding of why some courses of action were selected and not others.

DEVELOPING A BROAD BASE OF SUPPORT

Without endorsement from agency executives and board members, funding organization administrators, and volunteers, no priority system is going to be used. No matter how highly refined the procedures or the quality of information used to generate the priorities, the product will be ignored unless the views of these people are incorporated into the needs assessment process.

There are two methods of building support for needs assess

ment. One is to create a needs assessment committee that is representative. The other is frequent consultation with the constituents of the needs assessment group. With respect to representation, agency executives and board members should be amply represented. Having half the needs assessment group composed of agency executives is not out of line, since they have the most to gain or lose from the process. We had the local agency executive association select the representatives rather than appoint them directly, which added to the representativeness of the group. The funding organizations also selected their own representatives. Only a small number are needed. In our case, we had one. Volunteers are the final element crucial to representativeness. Individuals should be selected who are going to be willing to give considerable time (for that is what it takes) and have a reputation for being independent (of both funders and agencies) and fair. Efforts should be made to obtain a cross-section of people so that minorities, various age categories, women, and areas of the community are represented. It is suggested that a unique group be created for the task, rather than assign needs assessment to an existing committee that will have already developed a history of alliances and special interests.

There are a number of critical points in the needs assessment process, where reviewing decisions with constituents is important. These are when (1) a list of needs is near final draft, (2) the process for assigning priorities to needs has been tentatively agreed upon, and (3) information that is to serve as the basis of priority decisions has been identified. If the process entails a major data collection effort, such as a community survey or interviews with agency executives, the data collection forms should be reviewed by constituents' groups as well.

By review, it is meant that once the needs assessment committee has thought through and put together one of these components, consitutent groups should be presented the material and invited to comment. Attempts should be made to incorporate comments into the final product so long as they don't compromise the integrity of the project. Representatives from the needs assessment committee should meet with the agency executives association, planning groups, and funding organizations and encourage a thorough discussion of the materials. On some occasions, it may require rewriting and returning to the constituent group for another review. If little revision is anticipated, the second review may be handled by mail, asking anyone who has concerns to call by a particular date. Consensus is important to developing and maintaining support for the project.

DEVISING A LIST OF NEEDS

Developing a list of needs is one of the initial tasks of the needs assessment group. The list must not only reflect the wide range of needs that can be met by human service programs, but it must be possible to associate the needs on the list with operating human service programs. Needs for food, housing, clothing, health, protection, and knowledge are too general. Most agencies serve a majority of these needs in one way or the other and it is difficult for people to imagine such needs in the abstract.

A list of categories of people with particular needs is something the nonspecialist in human services can think about in specific terms. At the same time, it is important not to organize need statements around services as such lists quickly lend to turf battles with which the nonspecialist is not ready to cope.

The list of 26 needs devised for the Lincoln-Lancaster County project is shown as questions 1 through 26 of the interview schedule used for a community survey (the schedule is reprinted in this chapter). Framing the needs statements into questions that were to be asked of the public in a telephone survey gave the statements a clarity and succinct quality that made them easy to discuss. While this list may be a good place to start for communities just getting underway with needs assessment, revisions would be needed to make them more compatible with the characteristics of the community in which they would be used.

Linking the list of needs to human service programs was achieved in two steps. A staff member for the needs assessment group who was thoroughly familiar with all of the human services programs made the preliminary assignment. Regular needs assessment committee members were deliberately kept out of the program assignment process, so that when they were making judgments about needs, they did not have particular agencies or programs in mind which might influence their judgment. In the second step, individual agency directors received a list of their program assignments and were invited to make comments. Every attempt was made to obtain agreement on the need categories, and in almost every case, this was achieved. In some cases, individual meetings were held with agency representatives, after which changes were made in assignments.

INFORMATION NEEDED TO ASSIGN PRIORITIES TO NEEDS

Once there is agreement on a list of needs, the Needs Assessment Committee should decide on the information upon which they would like to base their priority assignments. The group must select information that is possible to obtain with limited funds and accept the idea that there will never be enough information. The authors propose a list of five questions around which information gathering for each need might be organized.

1. What part of the population has the need? Some grasp of the overall dimensions of the need is a useful baseline from which to start. This figure can then be compared with the number of those in need who feel that their need is unmet.
2. What part of the population is in need of increased services? In other words, what part of the population has all or part of this need unmet?
3. What are the consequences of not meeting the need? What is the impact on the community and the client of not meeting the need?
4. What are the community attitudes regarding the importance of the need? While the views of those in need is fundamental, what the public is willing to support is also important. Where the views of the needs and the public conflict, some balance must be achieved in order to have a stable and workable policy. Community attitudes on the importance of meeting the need and on whether more or less resources should be allocated to the need should be tapped.
5. What portion of the human service resources in (Name of Community) are being devoted to meet the need? In

assigning priorities, one needs to take into account what is already being done to meet the need.

Other information on each need may be important as well. The previous list is suggestive and not inclusive.

GATHERING INFORMATION

There are numerous sources of information. Some are more crucial and practical than others. *Agency executives* are perhaps the most important and valuable sources. They are in touch with the needs of the community on a daily basis and have at their fingertips information from their national association, data on their own agency's caseload, as well as other pertinent facts. Data on each of the five information areas described above can be obtained through a special human service agency executive questionnaire or interview. In the Lincoln-Lancaster project, the questions were asked as part of the budget application form. The specific questions used are as follows:

1. Population in need:
   What is the number of persons needing this program in (Name of Community)? This question misses information on needs not precisely reflected in existing programs. The question could be framed more generally, but the quality of the information would probably have been diminished because the agency executive would have less precise information.
2. Population with unmet need:
   What is the number of people in (Name of Community) whose needs are not being met either through your program or others?
3. Consequences of not meeting the need:
   What, in specific terms, would be the effect upon those persons being served if the program was greatly reduced or not available?
4. Community attitude:
   What is the public's attitude toward individuals in need of your agency's services? Would you say the public, in general, is deeply concerned, sympathetic, indifferent, disapproving, or antagonistic?

5. Resources:
   Add together program budget figures for all agencies serving clients with a particular need.

Whenever needs assessment committee resources allow it, information from agency executives should be supplemented with data from other sources. Each executive's information is limited. Even when pooled with other executives, it is incomplete and presented from the point of view of someone trying to maximize resources. In the Lincoln-Lancaster County project, agency director information was supplemented by a telephone interview survey of the noninstitutionalized adult population in the area. Social surveys enjoy a fair amount of credibility and can provide reliable information on four of the five areas noted above. Refer to the appropriate questions in the interview schedule on pages 145-167.

1. Population in need:
   Responses to question C indicate whether someone in the household is in need. The percent of the respondents answering yes can be multiplied by the number of households in the area (according to the most recent Census estimate) to get an idea of the number of households inhabited by someone with a particular need.
2. Population with unmet needs:
   This figure can be obtained by using answers to questions B and C. Among the respondents indicating someone in their household has a particular need, the percent who believe that resources should be increased can be multiplied by the number of households derived in point number 1 above. Those in need who believe resources should be increased probably have unmet needs. One could also take the proportion of local service users (question D) who believe resources should be increased as an indicator of unmet needs. Presumably those not using local resources or who feel resources allocation is sufficient have no unmet needs.
3. Community attitudes:
   Responses to questions A and B can be used to estimate community support for human services in each need area. The percent of respondents who view the need as "very

important" (question A) is one indicator of support. Another is the percent who believe resources should be increased to meet the need (question B). One could turn the figures around and calculate the lack of support for each need. Finally, one could combine the answers to A and B by calculating the percent of the respondents who think the need is "very important," and who also believe resources should be increased to meet the need.

4. Resources:
The information on total budget allocations derived from agency executives or public records for each need could be combined with the number of households using local services (question D) to derive a dollars-per-family-in-need figure. Such information may be more useful than the total budget figure by itself.

ID __ __ __   0103
DATE _____ TIME __ : __
Interviewed by _____   __ __   0405
Validated by _____

HUMAN SERVICE PROGRAMS ATTITUDE STUDY

HELLO, my name is _____ . We are conducting an attitude study for the City of Lincoln, Lancaster County and United Way. The purpose is to get peoples' opinions of how donated and tax dollars should be spent on needed human services.

INTERVIEWER NOTE: The committee doing the study is the Attitude Assessment Committee on behalf of the City of Lincoln, Lancaster County and United Way. For further information, please contact (Name of person who can answer queries).

In order for our study to reflect the attitudes of everyone age 18 or older, I will want to select someone at random from your household to interview.

SQ 1. Could you tell me how many individuals in your household are age 18 or older?   _____

SQ 2. And they are? (List names or relationships in order mentioned)

(Obtain person to talk to from the selection table based on number of individuals age 18 or older in the household)

SQ 3. Please may I speak to _____ ? (From above list)

(If not available, make an appointment)

PHONE NUMBER: __ __ __ __ __ __ __   0612

Now I'm going to mention some types of people who may be in need of human services. After I mention each type, I want you to tell me how important you feel it is that these needs be met and whether you feel resources allocated to meet these needs should be increased or decreased. Keep in mind that because of hard times some human services may have to be cut.

Please: Rotate Questions 1 thru 26 (By page)

1. Disaster victims and low-income persons who need emergency assistance, such as clothing, furniture, food, home heating fuel or gasoline.

   A. Would you say providing human services to meet this need in Lincoln and Lancaster County is:

	Very Important	... 1	13
	Somewhat Important	... 2	
	Not Very Important	... 3	
	(DK)	... 8	
	(Refused)	... 9	

   B. Should the resources allocated to meet these needs be:

	Increased	... 1	14
	Kept About the Same	... 2	
	Decreased	... 3	
	(DK)	... 8	
	(Refused)	... 9	

   C. Are these needs felt by yourself or someone in your household?

	Yes	... 1	15
(Skip to 2)	No	... 2	
(Skip to 2)	(DK)	... 8	
(Skip to 2)	(Refused)	... 9	

   D. Are you using local services to help meet these needs?

	Yes	... 1	16
	No	... 2	
	(DK)	... 8	
	(Refused)	... 9	

2. Individuals in need of employment or volunteer opportunities whose needs might be met by counseling, training or work experience.

   A. Would you say providing human services to meet this need in Lincoln and Lancaster County is:

	Very Important	... 1	17
	Somewhat Important	... 2	
	Not Very Important	... 3	
	(DK)	... 8	
	(Refused)	... 9	

B. Should the resources allocated to meet these needs be:

Increased ... 1 18
Kept About the Same ... 2
Decreased ... 3
(DK) ... 8
(Refused) ... 9

C. Are these needs felt by yourself or someone in your household?

Yes ... 1 19
(Skip to 3)   No ... 2
(Skip to 3)   (DK) ... 8
(Skip to 3)   (Refused) ... 9

D. Are you using local services to help meet these needs?

Yes ... 1 20
No ... 2
(DK) ... 8
(Refused) ... 9

3. Individuals unable to meet the cost of retaining a private attorney who need legal assistance.

A. Would you say providing human services to meet this need in Lincoln and Lancaster County is:

Very Important ... 1 21
Somewhat Important ... 2
Not Very Important ... 3
(DK) ... 8
(Refused) ... 9

B. Should the resources allocated to meet these needs be:

Increased ... 1 22
Kept About the Same ... 2
Decreased ... 3
(DK) ... 8
(Refused) ... 9

C. Are these needs felt by yourself or someone in your household?

Yes ... 1 23
(Skip to 4)   No ... 2
(Skip to 4)   (DK) ... 8
(Skip to 4)   (Refused) ... 9

D. Are you using local services to help meet these needs?

                                        Yes ... 1   24
                                         No ... 2
                                       (DK) ... 8
                                  (Refused) ... 9

4. People who need special transportation, such as the elderly or the handicapped.

   A. Would you say providing human services to meet this need in Lincoln and Lancaster County is:

                               Very Important ... 1   25
                           Somewhat Important ... 2
                           Not Very Important ... 3
                                       (DK) ... 8
                                  (Refused) ... 9

   B. Should the resources allocated to meet these needs be:

                                   Increased ... 1   26
                         Kept About the Same ... 2
                                   Decreased ... 3
                                       (DK) ... 8
                                  (Refused) ... 9

   C. Are these needs felt by yourself or someone in your household?

                                        Yes ... 1   27
                    (Skip to 5)   No ... 2
                    (Skip to 5)   (DK) ... 8
                    (Skip to 5)   (Refused) ... 9

   D. Are you using local services to help meet these needs?

                                        Yes ... 1   28
                                         No ... 2
                                       (DK) ... 8
                                  (Refused) ... 9

5. Individuals who need advice on where to go for help.

   A. Would you say providing human services to meet this need in Lincoln and Lancaster County is:

                               Very Important ... 1   29
                           Somewhat Important ... 2
                           Not Very Important ... 3
                                       (DK) ... 8
                                  (Refused) ... 9

B. Should the resources allocated to meet these needs be:

Increased ... 1 30
Kept About the Same ... 2
Decreased ... 3
(DK) ... 8
(Refused) ... 9

C. Are these needs felt by yourself or someone in your household?

Yes ... 1 31
(Skip to 6) No ... 2
(Skip to 6) (DK) ... 8
(Skip to 6) (Refused) ... 9

D. Are you using local services to help meet these needs?

Yes ... 1 32
No ... 2
(DK) ... 8
(Refused) ... 9

6. Families, adults and children who need counseling to help them deal with their problems.

A. Would you say providing human services to meet this need in Lincoln and Lancaster County is:

Very Important ... 1 33
Somewhat Important ... 2
Not Very Important ... 3
(DK) ... 8
(Refused) ... 9

B. Should the resources allocated to meet these needs be:

Increased ... 1 34
Kept About the Same ... 2
Decreased ... 3
(DK) ... 8
(Refused) ... 9

C. Are these needs felt by yourself or someone in your household?

Yes ... 1 35
(Skip to 7) No ... 2
(Skip to 7) (DK) ... 8
(Skip to 7) (Refused) ... 9

D. Are you using local services to help meet these needs?

Yes ...	1	36
No ...	2	
(DK) ...	8	
(Refused) ...	9	

7. Children in need of an adoption or foster care.

A. Would you say providing human services to meet this need in Lincoln and Lancaster County is:

Very Important ...	1	37
Somewhat Important ...	2	
Not Very Important ...	3	
(DK) ...	8	
(Refused) ...	9	

B. Should the resources allocated to meet these needs be:

Increased ...	1	38
Kept About the Same ...	2	
Decreased ...	3	
(DK) ...	8	
(Refused) ...	9	

C. Are these needs felt by yourself or someone in your household?

	Yes ...	1	39
(Skip to 8)	No ...	2	
(Skip to 8)	(DK) ...	8	
(Skip to 8)	(Refused) ...	9	

D. Are you using local services to help meet these needs?

Yes ...	1	40
No ...	2	
(DK) ...	8	
(Refused) ...	9	

8. Children who need care while their parents are working or going to school.

A. Would you say providing human services to meet this need in Lincoln and Lancaster County is:

Very Important ...	1	41
Somewhat Important ...	2	
Not Very Important ...	3	
(DK) ...	8	
(Refused) ...	9	

B. Should the resources allocated to meet these needs be:

Increased ... 1   42
Kept About the Same ... 2
Decreased ... 3
(DK) ... 8
(Refused) ... 9

C. Are these needs felt by yourself or someone in your household?

Yes ... 1   43
(Skip to 9)   No ... 2
(Skip to 9)   (DK) ... 8
(Skip to 9)   (Refused) ... 9

D. Are you using local services to help meet these needs?

Yes ... 1   44
No ... 2
(DK) ... 8
(Refused) ... 9

9. Children needing protection because they are abused or neglected.

A. Would you say providing human services to meet this need in Lincoln and Lancaster County is:

Very Important ... 1   45
Somewhat Important ... 2
Not Very Important ... 3
(DK) ... 8
(Refused) ... 9

B. Should the resources allocated to meet these needs be:

Increased ... 1   46
Kept About the Same ... 2
Decreased ... 3
(DK) ... 8
(Refused) ... 9

C. Are these needs felt by yourself or someone in your household?

Yes ... 1   47
(Skip to 10)   No ... 2
(Skip to 10)   (DK) ... 8
(Skip to 10)   (Refused) ... 9

D. Are you using local services to help meet these needs?

                        Yes ... 1   48
                        No ... 2
                    (DK) ... 8
               (Refused) ... 9

10. Elderly who are in need of a place to get together with other people, hot meals, or counseling to help them live independently.

   A. Would you say providing human services to meet this need in Lincoln and Lancaster County is:

                  Very Important ... 1   49
              Somewhat Important ... 2
              Not Very Important ... 3
                          (DK) ... 8
                     (Refused) ... 9

   B. Should the resources allocated to meet these needs be:

                      Increased ... 1   50
            Kept About the Same ... 2
                      Decreased ... 3
                          (DK) ... 8
                     (Refused) ... 9

   C. Are these needs felt by yourself or someone in your household?

                                Yes ... 1   51
         (Skip to 11)   No ... 2
         (Skip to 11)   (DK) ... 8
         (Skip to 11)   (Refused) ... 9

   D. Are you using local services to help meet these needs?

                        Yes ... 1   52
                        No ... 2
                    (DK) ... 8
               (Refused) ... 9

11. Children and youth needing residential care because they are pregnant, in trouble with the law, have run away from home or face other personal crises.

    A. Would you say providing human services to meet this need in Lincoln and Lancaster County is:

Very Important ... 1   53
Somewhat Important ... 2
Not Very Important ... 3
(DK) ... 8
(Refused) ... 9

    B. Should be resources allocated to meet these needs be:

Increased ... 1   54
Kept About the Same ... 2
Decreased ... 3
(DK) ... 8
(Refused) ... 9

    C. Are these needs felt by yourself or someone in your household?

Yes ... 1   55
(Skip to 12)   No ... 2
(Skip to 12)   (DK) ... 8
(Skip to 12)   (Refused) ... 9

    D. Are you using local services to help meet these needs?

Yes ... 1   56
No ... 2
(DK) ... 8
(Refused) ... 9

12. Adults and families needing temporary shelter, such as the homeless, transients and others.

    A. Would you say providing human services to meet this need in Lincoln and Lancaster County is:

Very Important ... 1   57
Somewhat Important ... 2
Not Very Important ... 3
(DK) ... 8
(Refused) ... 9

B. Should the resources allocated to meet these needs be:

Increased ... 1 58
Kept About the Same ... 2
Decreased ... 3
(DK) ... 8
(Refused) ... 9

C. Are these needs felt by yourself or someone in your household?

                           Yes ... 1 59
(Skip to 13)   No ... 2
(Skip to 13)   (DK) ... 8
(Skip to 13) (Refused) ... 9

D. Are you using local services to help meet these needs?

Yes ... 1 60
No ... 2
(DK) ... 8
(Refused) ... 9

13. Adults and children with severe mental or emotional problems who need treatment, special housing or job training and placement.

A. Would you say providing human services to meet this need in Lincoln and Lancaster County is:

Very Important ... 1 61
Somewhat Important ... 2
Not Very Important ... 3
(DK) ... 8
(Refused) ... 9

B. Should the resources allocated to meet these needs be:

Increased ... 1 62
Kept About the Same ... 2
Decreased ... 3
(DK) ... 8
(Refused) ... 9

C. Are these needs felt by yourself or someone in your household?

                           Yes ... 1 63
(Skip to 14)   No ... 2
(Skip to 14)   (DK) ... 8
(Skip to 14) (Refused) ... 9

D. Are you using local services to help meet these needs?

Yes ... 1   64
No ... 2
(DK) ... 8
(Refused) ... 9

14. Drug or alcohol dependent persons who need treatment in a residential setting, rehabilitation, counseling or emergency assistance.

A. Would you say providing human services to meet this need in Lincoln and Lancaster County is:

Very Important ... 1   65
Somewhat Important ... 2
Not Very Important ... 3
(DK) ... 8
(Refused) ... 9

B. Should the resources allocated to meet these needs be:

Increased ... 1   66
Kept About the Same ... 2
Decreased ... 3
(DK) ... 8
(Refused) ... 9

C. Are these needs felt by yourself or someone in your household?

Yes ... 1   67
(Skip to 15)   No ... 2
(Skip to 15)   (DK) ... 8
(Skip to 15)   (Refused) ... 9

D. Are you using local services to help meet these needs?

Yes ... 1   68
No ... 2
(DK) ... 8
(Refused) ... 9

15. Mentally retarded individuals who need job training or placement, special housing, rehabilitation services or counseling.

A. Would you say providing human services to meet this need in Lincoln and Lancaster County is:

Very Important ... 1   69
Somewhat Important ... 2
Not Very Important ... 3
(DK) ... 8
(Refused) ... 9

B. Should the resources allocated to meet these needs be:

$$
\begin{array}{llll}
& \text{Increased} & \text{...} & 1 & 70 \\
\text{Kept About the Same} & \text{...} & 2 \\
& \text{Decreased} & \text{...} & 3 \\
& \text{(DK)} & \text{...} & 8 \\
& \text{(Refused)} & \text{...} & 9
\end{array}
$$

C. Are these needs felt by yourself or someone in your household?

```
                              Yes ... 1   71
(Skip to 16)         No ... 2
(Skip to 16)       (DK) ... 8
(Skip to 16)  (Refused) ... 9
```

D. Are you using local services to help meet these needs?

```
              Yes ... 1   72
              No ... 2
            (DK) ... 8
        (Refused) ... 9
```

16. Low-income people in need of help to pay for their housing or housing improvements.

A. Would you say providing human services to meet this need in Lincoln and Lancaster County is:

```
     Very Important ... 1   73
 Somewhat Important ... 2
 Not Very Important ... 3
              (DK) ... 8
          (Refused) ... 9
```

B. Should the resources allocated to meet these needs be:

```
          Increased ... 1   74
Kept About the Same ... 2
          Decreased ... 3
               (DK) ... 8
           (Refused) ... 9
```

C. Are these needs felt by yourself or someone in your household?

```
                            Yes ... 1   75
(Skip to 17)         No ... 2
(Skip to 17)       (DK) ... 8
(Skip to 17) (Refused) ... 9
```

D. Are you using local services to help meet these needs?

Yes ... 1 76
No ... 2
(DK) ... 8
(Refused) ... 9

17. Low-income elderly in need of 24-hour nursing home care.

    A. Would you say providing human services to meet this need in Lincoln and Lancaster County is:

Very Important ... 1 77
Somewhat Important ... 2
Not Very Important ... 3
(DK) ... 8
(Refused) ... 9

    B. Should the resources allocated to meet these needs be:

Increased ... 1 78
Kept About the Same ... 2
Decreased ... 3
(DK) ... 8
(Refused) ... 9

Card #1 79

    C. Are these needs felt by yourself or someone in your household?

Yes ... 1 04
(Skip to 18)   No ... 2
(Skip to 18)   (DK) ... 8
(Skip to 18)   (Refused) ... 9

    D. Are you using local services to help meet these needs?

Yes ... 1 05
No ... 2
(DK) ... 8
(Refused) ... 9

18. Children and youth needing supervision, positive role models, group experiences and other healthy outlets that encourage youth development or delinquency prevention.

    A. Would you say providing human services to meet this need in Lincoln and Lancaster County is:

                                Very Important ... 1   06
                           Somewhat Important ... 2
                         Not Very Important ... 3
                                     (DK) ... 8
                            (Refused) ... 9

    B. Should the resources allocated to meet these needs be:

                                  Increased ... 1   07
                      Kept About the Same ... 2
                              Decreased ... 3
                                     (DK) ... 8
                            (Refused) ... 9

    C. Are these needs felt by yourself or someone in your household?

                                        Yes ... 1   08
       (Skip to 19)   No ... 2
       (Skip to 19)   (DK) ... 8
       (Skip to 19)   (Refused) ... 9

    D. Are you using local services to help meet these needs?

                                        Yes ... 1   09
                                       No ... 2
                                     (DK) ... 8
                              (Refused) ... 9

19. Individuals of all ages who need recreational, social and personal growth opportunities for the prevention of social and behavior problems.

    A. Would you say providing human services to meet this need in Lincoln and Lancaster County is:

                                Very Important ... 1   10
                           Somewhat Important ... 2
                         Not Very Important ... 3
                                     (DK) ... 8
                            (Refused) ... 9

B. Should the resources allocated to meet these needs be:

$$\begin{array}{ll}
\text{Increased} \dots \text{1} & \text{11} \\
\text{Kept About the Same} \dots \text{2} & \\
\text{Decreased} \dots \text{3} & \\
\text{(DK)} \dots \text{8} & \\
\text{(Refused)} \dots \text{9} &
\end{array}$$

C. Are these needs felt by yourself or someone in your household?

	Yes ... 1	12
(Skip to 20)	No ... 2	
(Skip to 20)	(DK) ... 8	
(Skip to 20)	(Refused) ... 9	

D. Are you using local services to help meet these needs?

$$\begin{array}{ll}
\text{Yes} \dots \text{1} & \text{13} \\
\text{No} \dots \text{2} & \\
\text{(DK)} \dots \text{8} & \\
\text{(Refused)} \dots \text{9} &
\end{array}$$

20. People who need help in recognizing and coping with relatives or co-workers who abuse drugs or alcohol, suffer from mental illness or have other problems.

A. Would you say providing human services to meet this need in Lincoln and Lancaster County is:

$$\begin{array}{ll}
\text{Very Important} \dots \text{1} & \text{14} \\
\text{Somewhat Important} \dots \text{2} & \\
\text{Not Very Important} \dots \text{3} & \\
\text{(DK)} \dots \text{8} & \\
\text{(Refused)} \dots \text{9} &
\end{array}$$

B. Should the resources allocated to meet these needs be:

$$\begin{array}{ll}
\text{Increased} \dots \text{1} & \text{15} \\
\text{Kept About the Same} \dots \text{2} & \\
\text{Decreased} \dots \text{3} & \\
\text{(DK)} \dots \text{8} & \\
\text{(Refused)} \dots \text{9} &
\end{array}$$

C. Are these needs felt by yourself or someone in your household?

	Yes ... 1	16
(Skip to 21)	No ... 2	
(Skip to 21)	(DK) ... 8	
(Skip to 21)	(Refused) ... 9	

D. Are you using local services to help meet these needs?

> Yes ... 1   17
> No ... 2
> (DK) ... 8
> (Refused) ... 9

21. People in need of health information, prevention services, or health care because they are sick.

    A. Would you say providing human services to meet this need in Lincoln and Lancaster County is:

> Very Important ... 1   18
> Somewhat Important ... 2
> Not Very Important ... 3
> (DK) ... 8
> (Refused) ... 9

    B. Should the resources allocated to meet these needs be:

> Yes ... 1   19
> Kept About the Same ... 2
> Decreased ... 3
> (DK) ... 8
> (Refused) ... 9

    C. Are these needs felt by yourself or someone in your household?

>   Yes ... 1   20
> (Skip to 22)   No ... 2
> (Skip to 22)   (DK) ... 8
> (Skip to 22) (Refused) ... 9

    D. Are you using local services to help meet these needs?

> Yes ... 1   21
> No ... 2
> (DK) ... 8
> (Refused) ... 9

22. Individuals who need in-home assistance with bathing, house cleaning or meals in order to live independently.

    A. Would you say providing human services to meet this need in Lincoln and Lancaster County is:

                                      Very Important ... 1 22
                        Somewhat Important ... 2
                        Not Very Important ... 3
                                        (DK) ... 8
                              (Refused) ... 9

    B. Should the resources allocated to meet these needs be:

                                        Increased ... 1 23
                    Kept About the Same ... 2
                            Decreased ... 3
                                    (DK) ... 8
                              (Refused) ... 9

    C. Are these needs felt by yourself or someone in your household?

                                        Yes ... 1 24
        (Skip to 23)   No ... 2
        (Skip to 23)   (DK) ... 8
        (Skip to 23) (Refused) ... 9

    D. Are you using local services to help meet these needs?

                                        Yes ... 1 25
                                        No ... 2
                                      (DK) ... 8
                            (Refused) ... 9

23. People such as children or the disabled who need someone to act on their behalf to ensure that they are treated fairly and receive the services to which they are entitled.

    A. Would you say providing human services to meet this need in Lincoln and Lancaster County is:

                                        Very Important ... 1 26
                        Somewhat Important ... 2
                        Not Very Important ... 3
                                        (DK) ... 8
                              (Refused) ... 9

B. Should the resources allocated to meet these needs be:

$$\begin{array}{r}\text{Increased} \ ... \ 1 \quad 27 \\ \text{Kept About the Same} \ ... \ 2 \\ \text{Decreased} \ ... \ 3 \\ \text{(DK)} \ ... \ 8 \\ \text{(Refused)} \ ... \ 9\end{array}$$

C. Are these needs felt by yourself or someone in your household?

$$\begin{array}{rr}& \text{Yes} \ ... \ 1 \quad 28 \\ \text{(Skip to 24)} & \text{No} \ ... \ 2 \\ \text{(Skip to 24)} & \text{(DK)} \ ... \ 8 \\ \text{(Skip to 24)} & \text{(Refused)} \ ... \ 9\end{array}$$

D. Are you using local services to help meet these needs?

$$\begin{array}{r}\text{Yes} \ ... \ 1 \quad 29 \\ \text{No} \ ... \ 2 \\ \text{(DK)} \ ... \ 8 \\ \text{(Refused)} \ ... \ 9\end{array}$$

24. Physically disabled individuals who need job training or placement, special equipment, in-home nursing care or help to live independently.

A. Would you say providing human services to meet this need in Lincoln and Lancaster County is:

$$\begin{array}{r}\text{Very Important} \ ... \ 1 \quad 30 \\ \text{Somewhat Important} \ ... \ 2 \\ \text{Not Very Important} \ ... \ 3 \\ \text{(DK)} \ ... \ 8 \\ \text{(Refused)} \ ... \ 9\end{array}$$

B. Should the resources allocated to meet these needs be:

$$\begin{array}{r}\text{Increased} \ ... \ 1 \quad 31 \\ \text{Kept About the Same} \ ... \ 2 \\ \text{Decreased} \ ... \ 3 \\ \text{(DK)} \ ... \ 8 \\ \text{(Refused)} \ ... \ 9\end{array}$$

C. Are these needs felt by yourself of someone in your household?

$$\begin{array}{rr}& \text{Yes} \ ... \ 1 \quad 32 \\ \text{(Skip to 25)} & \text{No} \ ... \ 2 \\ \text{(Skip to 25)} & \text{(DK)} \ ... \ 8 \\ \text{(Skip to 25)} & \text{(Refused)} \ ... \ 9\end{array}$$

D. Are you using local services to help meet these needs?

                              Yes ... 1 33
                               No ... 2
                            (DK) ... 8
                      (Refused) ... 9

25. Persons facing personal problems, such as divorce, domestic abuse, unwanted pregnancy, crime victimization, rape or suicide who need crisis assistance or counseling.

A. Would you say providing human services to meet this need in Lincoln and Lancaster County is:

                   Very Important ... 1 34
               Somewhat Important ... 2
               Not Very Important ... 3
                            (DK) ... 8
                      (Refused) ... 9

B. Should the resources allocated to meet these needs be:

                        Increased ... 1 35
            Kept About the Same ... 2
                       Decreased ... 3
                            (DK) ... 8
                      (Refused) ... 9

C. Are these needs felt by yourself or someone in your household?

                              Yes ... 1 36
        (Skip to 26)   No ... 2
        (Skip to 26)   (DK) ... 8
        (Skip to 26) (Refused) ... 9

D. Are you using local services to help meet these needs:

                              Yes ... 1 37
                               No ... 2
                            (DK) ... 8
                      (Refused) ... 9

26. Women, minorities and others who have been discriminated against in employment, housing, or other areas who need legal assistance, job training or counseling.

A. Would you say providing human services to meet this need in Lincoln and Lancaster County is:

Very Important ... 1 38
Somewhat Important ... 2
Not Very Important ... 3
(DK) ... 8
(Refused) ... 9

B. Should the resources allocated to meet these needs be:

Increased ... 1 39
Kept About the Same ... 2
Decreased ... 3
(DK) ... 8
(Refused) ... 9

C. Are these needs felt by yourself or someone in your household?

Yes ... 1 40
(Skip to 27) No ... 2
(Skip to 27) (DK) ... 8
(Skip to 27) (Refused) ... 9

D. Are you using local services to help meet these needs?

Yes ... 1 41
No ... 2
(DK) ... 8
(Refused) ... 9

The last few questions are needed for classifying responses and are strictly confidential and voluntary.

---

27. Sex: (Do not ask, just record)

Male ... 1 42
Female ... 2

28. What is your age:

Age __ __ 4344

29. Could you please tell me the number of people
living in your household, including yourself,
in each of these age groups:

A.	6 and under	___	45
B.	7 to 18	___	46
C.	19 to 30	___	47
D.	31 to 45	___	48
E.	46 to 60	___	49
F.	Over 60	___	50

30. Last week, were you working full-time, part-time, going
to school, keeping house, or what?

Working full-time (35 hrs. or more) ... 01   5152
Working part-time (1 to 34 hrs.) ... 02
Has a job but not working (vac., ill, etc.) ... 03
Unemployed, laid off, looking for work ... 04
Retired ... 05
In School ... 06
Keeping house ... 07
Other (Please specify_____) ... 08
(DK) ... 98
(Refused) ... 99

31. What is the highest level of education you
happened to complete?

Less than high school ... 1   53
High school graduate ... 2
Some college ... 3
College graduate ... 4
Graduate work ... 5
(Refused) ... 9

32. Do you consider yourself to be a member of
a racial or ethnic minority group?

Yes ... 1   54
(Skip to 34) No ... 2
(Skip to 34) (Refused) ... 9

33. (If yes) Which minority?

Black/Negro ... 1   55
Chicano/Mexican/Hispanic ... 2
American Indian/Native American ... 3
Oriental ... 4
Other (Please specify _____) ... 5

34. Do you live within the Lincoln city limits?

Yes ... 1   56
(Skip to 35) No ... 2

   A. (If yes) Do you live north or south
   of "O" Street?

North ... 1   57
South ... 2

   B. (If yes) Do you live west or east of
      27th Street?

                                             West ... 1   58
                                             East ... 2

35. Last year, was your total household income,
    including all wage earners,*under* or
    over $20,000 per year?

                                            Under ... 1   59
                                             Over ... 2
                          (Skip to 36) (DK) ... 8
                     (Skip to 36) (Refused) ... 9

      A. I am going to mention a number of
         income categories. When I mention
         the category which best describes
         your total household income for last
         year, please stop me.
         (Read the following if income is less
         than $20,000)

                                 Under $5,000 ... 1   60
                              $5,000 - $9,999 ... 2
                            $10,000 - $14,999 ... 3
                            $15,000 - $19,999 ... 4
                                        (DK) ... 8
                                   (Refused) ... 9

         (Read the following if income is
         $20,000 or more)

                            $20,000 - $24,999 ... 1   61
                            $25,000 - $29,999 ... 2
                            $30,000 - $39,999 ... 3
                            $40,000 - $49,999 ... 4
                            $50,000 - $59,999 ... 5
                              $60,000 or more ... 6
                                        (DK) ... 8
                                   (Refused) ... 9

36. Are you currently single, married, separated,
    divorced, widowed or what?

                                           Single ... 1   62
                                          Married ... 2
                                        Separated ... 3
                                         Divorced ... 4
                                         Widowed ... 5
                                            Other ... 6
                                        (Refused) ... 9

37. In order to help locate human service facilities
    where they will be most convenient to those
    who use them, I would like to know your zip code.
                        ZIP CODE _ _ _ _ _   6367
                                 Card #2   68

> This concludes our questions. Do you have any questions that you would like to ask me, or comments about this research project?
>
> Thank you for participating.
> G O O D B Y E

The authors found a sample size of 600 respondents sufficient to tap the 26 needs. If the results of the survey were going to be used for purposes requiring more precision, a larger sample would be called for. The sampling error is well within tolerable bounds (from ± 3%, depending on the size of the figure being used) for the needs assessment process described below.

The disadvantage of community surveys is that they are expensive. A sample of 600 generated using random digit dialing and interviewers using the schedule on the preceeding pages cost approximately $6,000 in 1983. In the Lincoln-Lancaster project, two reliable local marketing research firms submitted bids near this figure, and several other firms proposed higher fees. In the case of the higher bids, the sampling designs were more exotic than required for the needs assessment project. One could try to mount a survey using volunteers to reduce interviewing costs, but it is probably not worth it. Considerable training is required to get individuals ready to interview, and most volunteers will only be willing to put in a few hours; it is debilitating for those organizing the survey. And $6,000 is not a large sum when it is put into the context of the number of dollars allocated that will be based in part on the community survey.

Note that the interview schedule solicits background information on age, sex, education, income, residential areas, marital status, minority identity, household composition, and employment. These are useful in building profiles of families with different types of needs. In one survey, the authors asked whether the respondent was a United Way donor. This information has been used by campaign workers to show that many donors use human services and for building donor profiles to be used in planning advertising.

The prevention versus meeting immediate needs controversy

was aided by survey data. To assess support for preventive services, the question was asked:

> Do you think that human service dollars should only be spent on providing services for people with immediate needs, or do you think that human service dollars should also be spent on services directed towards the prevention of problems that give rise to these needs?

In the Lincoln-Lancaster County area, 79 percent favored spending on preventive programs.

With the emphasis on private funding for human services, one could glean valuable information by asking respondents, "Tell me if you feel the need should be supported mostly by tax dollars or mostly by donated dollars, or neither?" This would add considerably to the cost of the survey. The authors would not recommend including it unless there is extensive demand for the information.

As a vehicle for uncovering new needs, the community survey was not effective. In response to open-ended questions, respondents could not think of areas that are not already covered by the needs statements.

A *newspaper survey* has been used by the Lincoln-Lancaster County project, but without much success. An abbreviated version of the interview schedule was presented, along with a feature story in a Sunday edition of the local paper. People were encouraged to have input into the way human service dollars were to be spent. The newspaper approach was seen as a way to appease people who claim that because they were not contacted as part of the telephone survey, views of certain segments of the community were not represented. The response to the survey was disappointing. In one year, 74 were received, and in another year, 158. While the answers did not differ significantly from the telephone survey, this fact should not be interpreted to mean that the newspaper survey was representative. Readers tend to have more education and higher incomes than nonreaders. Those who completed the form were especially affluent and educated.

Sending questionnaires to community leaders is another way of obtaining information on human service needs. The officers of voluntary associations probably reflect the views of their members and represent a cadre of influential people whose views need to be considered. Experience indicates, however, that the return (even with follow-up phone calls) is low. Moreover, the views of such individuals are, no doubt, already reflected in the political processess that go into human service allocations.

Public meetings are a forum often used in formulating policy. These, too, have not been found to be effective in Lincoln-Lancaster County. Attendance is pitifully small (even after extensive publicity), and those who show up are human service representatives such as staff, board members, friends, and an occasional client. Usually, the clients were not representative of service users in general. Little new information has been gained through public meetings.

Client input is an important aspect of needs assessment, but this can best be brought into the needs assessment process by the agency executives and the community survey. Agency executives have close contact with clients (or at least their staff does), and they are usually the targets of client organizations where they exist. Public meetings designed to hear from clients, in our experience, were difficult to organize and poorly attended. Most of the participants had been "primed" by agency executives, and little information that was new was gained from the meetings. This is not to say that efforts should not be made to gain information from clients. When it is clear that client organizations want to appear before a needs assessment group, they should be given an opportunity to do so in a meeting or other appropriate forum. Unless clients are organized, it is the author's experience that their most effective channel to the needs assessment committee is agency staff and executives.

Once sources of information have been identified and the data collected, it should be put in summary form for each need so that members of the needs assessment committee can readily make use of it in their deliberations. The authors propose a one or two page summary form that contains all the information on a particular need. A model form that contains information from agency executives and a community telephone survey is presented on pages 170-172. Copies of the community survey interview schedule and agency executive questionnaire are also available, so that the member can refresh his/her memory about the way the information was obtained. On the form, under "agency executives," there is space to list information from four people who have responsibility for programs in the needs area. The form would have to be modified if there were more agencies in a particular need area. Individuals are never identified, nor are the programs. Respondents are identified by number. The last page of the form is for the needs assessment committee member to record his/her own rating and those of other committee members in the course of setting priorities. Use of this form will be described in more detail in the next section. The information summaries should be prepared by staff supporting the needs assessment committee, so that no committee member has unusual access to information that may bias their ratings.

Needs Assessment Summary Information
Description of Need:

1. NUMBER IN NEED   Percent in   Number of
   Community Survey: Need _____   Households _____
   Agency Executive: _____ _____   _____ _____
   Number of People: _____ _____   _____ _____

2. NUMBER WITH UNMET
   NEEDS   Percent With   Number of
   Community Survey: Unmet Need _____   Households _____
   Agency Executive: _____ _____   _____ _____
   Number of People: _____ _____   _____ _____

3. CONSEQUENCES OF NOT
   MEETING NEED
   Agency Executive: _____

   Agency Executive: _____

   Agency Executive: _____

   Agency Executive: _____

4. COMMUNITY ATTITUDE REGARDING IMPORTANCE OF NEED
   Community Survey:
   Percent of respondents who regard need as very important _____
   Percent of respondents who want to increase resources _____

   Agency Executive:
   Number who checked each category of community support
      Antagonistic __; Disapproving __; Indifferent __;
      Sympathetic __; Deeply Concerned __; No Answer __

5. PORTIONS OF HUMAN SERVICE RESOURCES ALLOCATED TO
   MEET NEED
   Total of *All* Human Service Programs reported $_____Grand Total
   Agency Executive ___ $_____; _____% of Grand Total
   Agency Executive ___ $_____; _____% of Grand Total
   Agency Executive ___ $_____; _____% of Grand Total
   Agency Executive ___ $_____; _____% of Grand Total
   Total allocated to meet this need:
                  $_____; _____% of Grand Total

Priority Assignments   .

Assign priority number as follows:

5 = very high priority	2 = low priority
4 = high priority	1 = very low priority
3 = moderate priority	

Use this space to record your assignment of priorities and that of each committee member.

	Your Rating	Other Member's Ratings
First Rating (done before meeting)	_____	___ ___ ___ ___ ___ ___ ___ ___ ___ ___ ___ ___ ___ ___ ___
Second Rating (if done)	_____	___ ___ ___ ___ ___ ___ ___ ___ ___ ___ ___ ___ ___ ___ ___
Third Rating (if done)	_____	___ ___ ___ ___ ___ ___ ___ ___ ___ ___ ___ ___ ___ ___ ___

Final Assignment _____

SETTING PRIORITIES

A series of at least four meetings should be scheduled within the space of three weeks. The close spacing of meetings enhances continuity. The first meeting is an orientation meeting where members of the needs assessment committee are given instructions on how they are to proceed, and are handed the information and forms needed to start. The second meeting should be scheduled about a week after the first to allow committee members plenty of time to read the materials and to do an independent assessment of needs. At the second and third meetings, members reveal their ratings, discuss them, and come to some consensus about a priority level for each need. The last meeting should be spent checking the priority ratings for balance and consistency, and on planning the way in which the priorities should be presented to the community.

After the orientation and before the first priority setting meeting, each committee member should set aside a period of several hours to review the information, think about the need, and without discussing it with others, assign a priority to it. It is crucial that each member do this, otherwise much of the value of subsequent meetings is lost because members have not given sufficient thought to needs. If possible, independent ratings should be a requirement for continued participation in the process. As a guide to making independent ratings, team members should be given the following instructions:

Instructions for Assigning Priorities Before
the Next Committee Meeting

1. Set aside two hours, during which ratings can be made in a setting where you won't be disturbed.
2. Assign a priority to each of the 26 need statements. Examine all five bits of information, weigh them, and assign a priority as follows: 5 = very high priority, 4 = high priority, 3 = moderate priority, 2 = low priority, 1 = very low priority.
3. Go through them once, quickly, using your best judgment and intuition. Do not get bogged down. If you are having trouble with one need, give it your "best guess" and go on.

4.   Use a pencil to record your priority on the "Priority Assignment" page attached to each needs' summary information form.

5.   If you wish, make notes defending your ratings as you go along. You may want to refer to them during committee meetings.

6.   Go through the needs again at a slower pace to see if what you have done holds together. Make any needed adjustments.

7.   After completing all 26 needs, transfer (in pencil) the ratings for each need to the Priority Rating Summary.

8.   Working from the summary, check the ratings you have made for balance. Ideally, you would have your ratings for 26 needs distributed as follows:

Priority

Very High	High	Moderate	Low	Very Low
3 (10%)	5 (20%)	10 (40%)	5 (20%)	3 (10%)

It may not be realistic to achieve such a balance. But, if your ratings are poorly balanced, go through the process of assigning priorities again so that the highs and lows are approximately equal in number.

9.   Again working from the summary, check your priority ratings for consistency. Look at all of the needs you have assigned to "very high" priority and see if they make sense as a group. Check each of the remaining four priority categories in the same way. Make adjustments as necessary.

10.   Stay with it until you get it done; it may be frustrating and you may not be totally satisfied with all of your assignments, but it is important that *everyone* complete all 26 needs.

11.   You may place more emphasis on some of the criteria than on others, but do so consistently for all 26 needs.

12.   *Do not* be thinking of specific agencies or programs when making your assignments. Try to discount personal associations and experiences that may bias your rating. Agency executives should not rank their own categories.

Priority Rating Summary

____ 1. Disaster victims and low-income persons who need emergency assistance, such as clothing, furniture, food, home heating fuel or gasoline.

____ 2. Individuals in need of employment or volunteer opportunities whose needs might be met by counseling, training or work experience.

____ 3. Individuals unable to meet the cost of retaining a private attorney who need legal assistance.

____ 4. People who need special transportation, such as the elderly or handicapped.

____ 5. Individuals who need advice on where to go for help.

____ 6. Families, adults and children who need counseling to help them deal with their problems.

____ 7. Children in need of an adoption or foster care.

____ 8. Children who need care while their parents are working or going to school.

____ 9. Children needing protection because they are abused or neglected.

____ 10. Elderly who are in need of a place to get together with other people, hot meals, or counseling to help them live independently.

____ 11. Children and youth needing residential care because they are pregnant, in trouble with the law, have run away from home or face other personal crises.

____ 12. Adults and families needing temporary shelter, such as the homeless, transients and others.

____ 13. Adults and children with severe mental or emotional problems who need treatment, special housing or job training and placement.

____ 14. Drug or alcohol dependent persons who need treatment in a residential setting, rehabilitation, counseling or emergency assistance.

____ 15. Mentally retarded individuals who need job training or placement, special housing, rehabilitation services or counseling.

____ 16. Low-income people in need of help to pay for their housing or housing improvements.

____ 17. Low-income elderly in need of 24-hour nursing home care.

____ 18. Children and youth needing supervision, positive role models, group experiences and other healthy outlets that encourage youth development or delinquency prevention.

____ 19. Individuals of all ages who need recreational, social and personal growth opportunities for the prevention of social and behavior problems.

____ 20. People who need help in recognizing and coping with relatives or co-workers who abuse drugs or alcohol, suffer from mental illness or have other problems.

_____ 21. People in need of health information, prevention services, or health care because they are sick.

_____ 22. Individuals who need in-home assistance with bathing, house cleaning or meals in order to live independently.

_____ 23. People such as children or the disabled who need someone to act on their behalf to ensure that they are treated fairly and receive the services to which they are entitled.

_____ 24. Physically disabled individuals who need job training or placement, special equipment, in-home nursing care or help to live independently.

_____ 25. Persons facing personal problems, such as divorce, domestic abuse, unwanted pregnancy, rape, crime victimization or suicide who need crisis assistance or counseling.

_____ 26. Women, minorites and others who have been discriminated against in employment, housing, or other areas who need legal assistance, job training or counseling.

At the next Needs Assessment Committee meetings, begin by dealing with each need in its entirety before going on to the next. In dealing with the first need, each person should reveal his/her priority assignment to the rest of the committee without comment. Each person has room on his/her Priority Assignments form to record the remainder of the committee's assignments. This record will give each person an overview of the consensus for that particular need. A staff member should keep an official record as well. If there is high consensus, solicit any comments anyone has. Give people a chance to change their assignments on the basis of the comments. Make another tabulation, and then assign the need priority given by the majority of members.

If there is little or no consensus, ask for members to defend their own particular assignment. After everyone has been heard from, entertain some general discussion and ask for everyone to make a second priority assignment. If there is consensus, assign the priority and move on to the next need.

If not, consider ways the need might be reformulated. Try to assign priorities to the reformulated need to see whether consensus emerges. If there is little or no consensus, ask for members to defend their own particular assignment. After everyone has been heard from, entertain some general discussion and ask everyone to make a second priority assignment. If there is consensus, assign the priority and move on to the next need. If all else fails, consider dropping the need from the list.

After going through the entire list of needs one at a time, the entire committee should examine the priority assignments for balance and consistency. If adjustment seems called for, adjustments should be made through formal action (motions and votes).

The Needs Assessment Committee may wish to collapse a category or two if there are too few (one or two) needs in it. There is nothing sacred about a five (four or any other number) category priority rating system. There is a problem in having too many priority ratings: for example, assigning a different priority level to all 26 needs. One can easily do this by adding together the committee members' final priority assignments. But to make distinctions between 26 needs on the basis of a point or two is a meaningless exercise. In doing so, one is making distinctions on the basis of very minor differences in opinion. Making such fine distinctions in this way will not have much credibility.

There are a number of mechanisms built into the process to keep self-interest from being reflected in the final product. The names of specific programs assigned to the need categories were absent from the information provided to the Committee. Committee members were asked to consider needs only and to refrain from discussing individual programs. Agency executives on the Committee were asked not to rank needs for which they provided service. All members were asked to acknowledge any conflict of interest they might have during discussion. These procedures seem to work well.

The presentation of the committee's work is an important aspect of the process. While the report need not be long, the presentation should include a thorough description of the entire process, so that there is no mystery as to how the priorities were derived. Methods that were used to reduce bias should be given special attention. A note of caution, in that the use of the priorities should be an integral part of the report. It might appear as follows:

> There are certain limitations within the needs assessment/priority-setting process that should be considered when using the results identified in the following pages. Readers are advised that the priorities outlined on the next page of this report are based on data collected

during the first quarter of 1983, reflecting services provided in 1982. As the priorities become older, their usefulness may diminish. Human needs change with time and the environment. It is important to remember that priorities identified today may change tomorrow.

Another major limitation of such procedures is that, by their very nature, they tend to over-simplify conditions. Every attempt has been made to present a comprehensive and descriptive list of human needs. However, the 26 human need statements constructed for this process cannot totally reflect the complexity of all human service needs, nor can they reflect the interrelationship among such needs.

It is not the intent of the Needs Assessment Committee that the priority need statements be used in isolation. Rather, they should be used in conjunction with other criteria for allocating resources. It should be further noted that no attempt was made to set priorities among the need statements within the four priority-tiers. Users of this report are urged to keep these limitations in mind. Any duplication of these priorities should contain these words of caution.

The list of needs that fall into each priority level should be presented as a group. Programs coordinate with each need may be listed under the need. Complete treatment of the priority-setting process in one report is important. The document can then be used as a reference for users of the priority study.

EVALUATION OF THE NEEDS ASSESSMENT PROCESS

After the first application of the human services priorities, the needs assessment process and use of the priorities should be evaluated. Such an evaluation gives the process additional credibility and sets the stage for subsequent needs assessments after the current one becomes dated.

The evaluation may be conducted, in many cases, by the needs assessment committee itself. If, however, there is a good deal of unrest, so that a self-evaluation would be suspect, it should be assigned to another group.

The evaluation committee should make attempts to gather information by (1) a questionnaire sent to funders (public and private) who might have used the priority ratings and to agency executives and (2) a public forum in which representatives of user groups and agency executives make presentations to the needs assessment committee, who are then invited to respond.

The questionnaire should be sent to all funders, agency executives, and planners who might have used the needs assessment study. A cover letter should explain the purpose of the study and give directions for completing the questionnaire. A deadline for return should be suggested. If the response is less than 50 percent, recipients should be called and nudged. If returns are still limited, some of the known users should be interviewed by phone to see if their responses would be different from those who have already returned the questionnaire. A sample questionnaire follows.

Needs Assessment Evaluation Questionnaire

I. Participants in the 1983 Human Services Planning Process

During 1983, several groups participated in the human services planning process. These groups included agencies affiliated with the Lancaster County Human Services Federation, local government officials, and the United Way.

A. Were there any interests not represented in the 1983 planning process that should have been?

Yes _____ No _____

If yes, who were they and how should they be asked to participate?

II. Needs Assessment Committee Membership and Size

The Needs Assessment Committee is responsible for the design and implementation of the Needs Assessment Study. Throughout the course of the 1981 Study, comments were solicited from human service agencies and local government officials. The actual assignment of priorities to the 26 human need statements was done by the Needs Assessment Committee, which was composed of (spell out representing, e.g., "seven Lancaster County Human Services Federation representatives, eight Planning Division representatives, and one Allocation Division representative.")

A. Were there any interests not represented on the 1981 Needs Assessment Committee that should have been?

Yes _____ No _____

If yes, who were they?

B. Were there interests on the Committee that were underrepresented?

Yes _____ No _____

If yes, who were they?

C. Were there interests represented on the Committee that should not have been?

Yes _____ No _____

If yes, who were they?

D. Do you feel the Needs Assessment Committee should increased in size, kept about the same size, or decreased in size?

_____a. Kept about the same
_____b. Increased in size to _____
_____c. Decreased in size to _____

If changes, what would be achieved by altering the size?

E. Do you feel that peoples' views were adequately solicited for each of the following aspects of the Needs Assessment Study?

Yes   No

a. Community Attitude Survey

   If no, please explain:

b. Agency Executive Information

   If no, please explain:

c. Devising and refining the 26
   needs statements

   If no, please explain:

III. The Twenty-Six Human Need Statements

   A. Recognizing that no one set of need statements will
      satisfy everyone concerned, we would like your sug-
      gestions for reformulating the 26 need categories.

      a. Should there be more need statements, fewer, or
         was the number about right?

      More _____ Fewer ___ About Right _____

      If more or less, what areas should be added or
      deleted?

   B. Do you have any other suggestions on the need
      categories? (e.g., content, emphasis, representative-
      ness)

                  Yes _____ No _____

   If yes, please make specific suggestions.

IV. The Needs Assessment Committee took five items of information into account when arriving at the priorities. They were

1. number in need
2. number with unmet needs
3. consequences of not meeting the need
4. community attitudes on importance of needs
5. portions of human service resources allocated to meet the need

A. Are there any other criteria that should be considered?

Yes _____ No _____

If yes, what are they?

B. Should any of the five criteria not be used in arriving at priorities?

Yes _____ No _____

If yes, which one(s) and why?

V. Is there any information that we should be asking agencies to provide as part of the Needs Assessment Study that we did not ask for in 1981?

Yes _____ No _____

If yes, please indicate information needed in specific terms.

VI. How important was each of the following in any success the Needs Assessment Study might have enjoyed?

	Very Important	Somewhat Important	Not Important	Very Important
A. Community Survey	_____	_____	_____	_____
B. Agency Executive Imformation	_____	_____	_____	_____
C. Agency representatives on key committees	_____	_____	_____	_____
D. Needs Assessment Committee review, deliberation and discussion of each need (consensus process)	_____	_____	_____	_____

VII. To what extent is the needs assessment product (the priorities) a good reflection of the community's human service needs as they existed in 1982?

Excellent   Very Good   Good   Not Too Good   Poor

VIII. Use of Priorities

There are a number of considerations that were taken into account during the process of making allocations to human service agencies for 1983. They include

-program productivity
-program effectiveness relative to others of a similar type
-whether or not the program is suffering unusual financial constraints due to changes in government spending
-the human services priorities
-technical matters of conformity to the regulations of funding bodies and estimates of revenue and expenditures.

A. Relative to the other allocations criteria, were the priorities

_____a. weighted too heavily
_____b. weighted just about right
_____c. not weighted enough

B. We would like to get your estimate about how much weight should be given to the human need priorities relative to other criteria. Listed below are four commonly used criteria. Leaving aside technical considerations, such as income and expense projections, assume that you have 100 points and assign the number of points to each of the criteria according to the amount of emphasis each should be given in the course of making allocations decisions. If you wish to add a fifth or sixth criterion and assign a weight to it, please do so. Be sure the points total to 100.

Criteria	Points
Program productivity	_____
Program effectiveness	_____
Unusual financial constraints	_____
Priority assignment	_____
_____	_____
_____	_____
	100 points

C. Do you have any other suggestions for utilization of the human need priorities in the allocations/budgeting process?

IX. Are you

_____ A member of the United Way Planning Division?
_____ A member of the United Way Allocations Cabinet?
_____ A member of the Joint Budget Committee?
_____ A human service agency director?

X. Please use the space below to give any other comments you may have about the needs assessment methodology and/or the use of the priorities.

THE FOLLOWING SECTION IS TO BE COMPLETED BY HUMAN SERVICE AGENCY DIRECTORS ONLY:

XI. Has anyone in your agency used information generated by needs assessment process?

                                            Yes   No

   A. Priorities Study   _____ _____

      If yes, explain how in specific terms:

   B. Community Attitude Survey   _____ _____

      If yes, explain how in specific terms:

    C. Agency Executive Information   _____ _____

       If yes, explain how in specific terms:

XII. Has the Priorities Study caused your agency to shift
     program emphasis at all?

                         Yes _____   No _____

     If yes, in what way? (e.g., client-groups, effects, etc.)

   The responses should be summarized, and the answers to open-
ended questions listed. The information should serve as the basis
for balanced judgments about the process and for recommendations about future needs assessment studies. A copy of the
questionnaire and the responses should be included as an
appendix to the report.
   While the questionnaires may be sufficient information upon
which to base an evaluation, the public forum allows for input
from individuals or groups who may have been missed. It is
important to arrange for reports from heavy-user groups (funders,
agency executive associations), so that the entire meeting is not
taken up by presentations from people who are not representative
of key groups. Minutes should be kept and, along with any reports
received, should be appended to the evaluation report.
   In the report, deal with every issue that is raised, whether it be
costs of the study, participation, methods used, representation,
use of the priorities, future needs assessments, quality of information, client input, or comprehensiveness. Summarize the infor-

mation pertinent to each issue, and then conclude with a recommendation. A draft of the final report should be reviewed by the Needs Assessment Committee and other key groups before final release. Providing the evaluation doesn't reveal a critical flaw in the needs assessment process, the evaluation will serve to increase use of the study. Wide distribution of the evaluation report is encouraged.

RECOMMENDATIONS FOR AGENCY EXECUTIVES

As suggested numerous times throughout the chapter, agency executive participation in the needs assessment process is crucial to the success of the effort. Therefore, agency directors should take an active role in (1) planning the needs assessment process, (2) providing high quality information upon which the needs assessment group can base priority assignments, (3) gaining representation on the group responsible for assessing needs, and (4) insuring that the priorities, once established, are not misused or poorly applied.

Priority studies can be used to strengthen applications for funds. When the funds being requested are for a high priority program, draw attention to this fact. Of course, it would not be sound management to completely overhaul one's programs to get them into high priority categories. Not only are the chances of it resulting in large increases in funding remote, but it puts proven programs at risk. Priority studies can more appropriately be used as a guide in planning new programs and as a guide to devising new ways to better serve existing clients.

Chapter 7

INTEGRATING HUMAN SERVICE PLANNING AND EVALUATION AT THE LOCAL LEVEL
A Case Study

INTRODUCTION

In "hard times," the idea of integrated planning may appear, at first glance, not to be a good use of limited resources. To have a community-wide program of planning and evaluation, as has been described in earlier chapters, may suggest to some another costly layer of bureaucracy. The experience in one community indicates that integrated planning and evaluation at the local level is cost-effective. If organized properly, integrated planning avoids duplication of planning efforts, provides better information upon which to base funding decisions, and paves the way for cost-effective interagency cooperation. In the pages that follow, the authors trace the efforts of one community that developed an integrated approach to human service planning and evaluation. They describe how it operates, some of the outcomes, and the factors found to be critical in getting such a project underway.

THE SETTING

The locality is the City of Lincoln, Nebraska, and the County in which it is located. The primary participants in the development of integrated planning were the Lancaster County Board of Commissioners, the mayor of Lincoln, the Lincoln City Council, and the United Way of Lincoln and Lancaster County. The county had a population of 192,884 in 1980 and has been growing at a modest and steady rate over the last two decades. The economic base is mixed, with dominate components being agribusiness, insurance, state government, and the University of Nebraska. While the number of registered Republicans and Democrats are about even, the politics are conservative. Occasionally, liberals get elected to the Board of Commissioners and City Council, but only rarely do they have a majority. Ethnically, the community is very homogenous and has enjoyed low unemployment rates (5%) even during recessions (8% was recorded during the 1982-83 decline). Nevertheless, the range of problems that call for human services programs is as great as found in most communities. While the proportion of the population effected is less than would be found in, say, the industrial cities of the Northeast, significant segments of the population are, nevertheless, in need of human services.

GETTING STARTED

The roots of the integrated planning program in Lincoln and Lancaster County may be traced to the large amount of Federal dollars coming under local control as a result of the State and Local Fiscal Assistance Act of 1972, and similar legislation. While many local governments used their windfall to obtain capital equipment, fix roads, and refurbish libraries, Lincoln's public officials, in 1973, chose to designate $400,000 of their general revenue sharing dollars to the support and development of human services.

Once that decision had been made, many other questions needed answering. How do we know which request to fund and for how much? What are the greatest needs in the community? How do we justify our decisions? How do we make sure that the money will be spent on what the applicant says? Should we fund management and other indirect costs, or should we just fund the direct costs of providing services? These and other questions surfaced as elected officials attempted to be equitable and consistent in the allocation of funds.

Having a history and process to deal with such questions, United Way offered to review and evaluate applications for revenue-sharing money. After much deliberation, the United Way offer was rejected by public officials on the grounds that taxpayers would object to having United Way telling elected officials how to spend tax generated money.

The mayor then hired a local consultant, who recommended that officials request United Way combine forces with two University-based research groups and develop a proposal for allocating funds. A proposal was prepared that defined human services on the basis of United Way of America Service Identification System, called for a community survey of needs, and outlined a process for allocating funds to old and new programs using teams of volunteers. This proposal, too, was rejected on the ground that such an effort might be interpreted by the public as an abrogation of elected officials' responsibility.

At about the same time, on the basis of another of the local consultant's recommendations, the City Council appointed a Human Services Advisory Committee comprised of a cross section of individuals, including an economics professor, an attorney, social workers, and a Veterans Administration administrator. This group recommended that the City Council and the County Board hire a human service administrator whose task it would be to advise elected officials on the above questions. This would assign the task to someone directly accountable to the elected officials, who would also provide year-round service. The Board and Council accepted the recommendation and hired a full-time human services administrator in 1975. Such City and County coordination was made easy by the City-County common (a committee established in 1973 consisting of representatives from both groups), which dealt with issues of mutual concern.

In 1976, United Way published its first human service needs study without assistance from either the City or the County. But the study group worked hard to keep the new human services administrator fully informed about every aspect of the study. The study rested on the work of nine task forces, each comprised of human service professionals, consumers, and volunteers. Each task force was organized around a separate issue, such as economic opportunity, housing, disaster relief, and so on. Using data already available from the 1970 Census and various human service agencies, the chairs of the task forces ranked needs into three different levels.

In 1978, the United Way/City-County Coordination Committee was formed. The Committee was not enfranchised with policy-setting or decision-making authority. Rather, it was to

serve as a monitor, checking the progress of the Planning
Division and making recommendations to its constituent policy-
making groups. Voting members of the Committee include the
mayor, Chair of the City Council, Chair of the County Board, and
United Way's President, Allocations Division Chair, and the
Planning Division Chair. Local foundations, School Board, and
representatives of local area human service agencys executive
associations are consistently invited to attend. The foundation
representatives have not been active participants until recently.
Staff assistance is provided both by United Way and the City-
County Human Service Administrator.

Based on the quality of the needs assessment study, the work of
the Coordination Committee, and the close working relationship
that the United Way executive director and the human services
administrator developed, the City, the County, and United Way
entered into a formal agreement in 1980. The agreement established the Planning Division of the United Way as the single
human services advisory body for the county-wide area. The
Planning Division was to assess needs and establish priorities. In
addition, they were to make recommendations and prepare
information at the request of any of the partners to the agreement.
The Planning Division was to serve the mayor, the City Council,
the County Board, and the United Way Board of Directors.

There is a good deal of planned turnover on the committee.
United Way representatives are elected each year, and there are
city council elections every two years. This does not seem
negatively to influence the effectiveness of the group. Once the
structure was in place, it seemed to serve as a liaison between the
principle parties in an effective way.

In 1980, the executives of human service agencies formed the
Lincoln-Lancaster County Human Services Federation. They
organized to make sure that their interests were fully represented
in the planning process and to conduct management seminars
and other events for their members. They appoint all agency
representatives to each needs assessment group and the representatives on agency evaluation teams. For every major change in
planning procedure and every new planning initiative, input is
solicited from this group. Sometimes it is through their representation on the Planning Division, and on other occasions (such as

mapping out the needs assessment process) the entire group is consulted regularly. Also, this Federation has managed to stimulate more extensive participation in contributing information to the needs assessment process and similar ventures.

The Planning Division has two basic operations: assessing human service needs and evaluating human service agencies. Between 1979 and 1983, human service needs have been assessed three times. Whether these studies will occur at the same pace in the future depends on the amount of change that seems to be occurring in the community. If little change is observed from one study to the next, studies may be less frequent. The last two needs assessment studies were built on the model described in detail in Chapter 6 and have enjoyed wide acceptance. The extent of their use by funding organizations is mixed. Priority studies never serve as the sole basis for funding decisions, but priority information is combined with other criteria, such as budget projections and agency effectiveness. As of 1983, the priority studies were not used consistently by all funding bodies. In some decisions the matter of priority never comes up, while in others it frames an important part of the discussion. The Planning Division is now working on developing uniform funding criteria that can be used by all human service funders in reviewing applications. Once adopted, need priorities would be used more systematically.

The other major function, program evaluation, is conducted annually. Each year, evaluation teams evaluate seven to ten different human service agencies. Given the number of agencies in the area, this means that each one is evaluated every four to five years. Some agencies, which have a human service component but whose major task is some other activity (for example, the Parks Department), are not evaluated. The limited resources are reserved for agencies whose primary goal is human service. The procedures used to evaluate agencies are modeled after processes described in Chapter 5. Every allocation group has a copy of the most recent evaluation at the time they review an agency's request. The parties that use the evaluation more than any other, however, are the agencies themselves. The recommendations coming from the evaluation are used extensively by the agencies in planning and managing their operation.

The Planning Division has also taken on special tasks that were thought to enhance human service planning. For example, in 1983, they undertook a study of methods agencies use to cope with declining resources. Agency executives were interviewed to obtain case studies of effective methods to cut expenses and raise revenues. Economists, businesspeople, and others outside the human services system were interviewed as well. The study was reported as a set of guidelines for Agency Executives. Management assistance workshops are also a regular activity of the Planning Division.

OUTCOMES OF INTEGRATED PLANNING

The integrated planning program in Lincoln and Lancaster County has provided a forum for the discussion of such critical issues as single versus multiple year funding, one year funding versus phased reduction of support, continuation versus zero-based budgeting versus percentage-of-base funding, and program versus agency funding. The coordinated planning effort has played a key role in the decision to switch from agency to program funding by all funding organizations.

Another product of the process is reduction of duplication of effort. For example, one application form is used by all agencies applying to United Way, the City, and the County. Thus, agencies seeking funds from multiple sources only need complete one set of forms. The various funding agencies do not carry out extensive separate planning activities. Except for special audits or reviews, only the Planning Division carries out agency evaluations. There are no separate efforts to assess needs and establish human service priorities.

The integrated approach to human service planning has also enhanced each funding body's public accountability. It supports the notion that allocations should be based on consistent criteria, community need, and program effectiveness, not on the basis of popularity, political pressure, or fad. The agencies also have an easier time demonstrating accountability as well. Program evaluations, for example, are used by agencies to show accountability to funders as well as other constituents, such as accreditation groups and citizen advisory groups.

The integrated planning process has facilitated coordinated

funding of projects. For example, Lindoln Goodwill Industries was going to lose all funding from the State, unless they could quickly implement plans to install a passenger elevator. This was necessary to make the upper floors of their building accessible to those with mobility limitations. Concerned staff and policymakers were able to put together a financial package that involved the City and County replacing United Way program subsidies to meet the deficit needs of Goodwill Industries for a year. This allowed United Way to shift its operational funding to provide the capital funds necessary to construct the elevator shaft and make other structural changes. A local foundation provided funds to buy the elevator cab and the mechanical equipment necessary for installation within the shaft. Following completion of this special project, United Way resumed its deficit financing role of operational costs, and the City-County and Lincoln Foundation concluded their funding relationship. Integrated planning fed directly and indirectly into these efforts. Directly, there is general agreement about the priorities, which leads to the common goal of funding the project. Indirectly, working together in planning means that the channels of communication between funders are open, and that there exists a tendency to want to cooperate on ventures other than planning.

Because City, County, and United Way financial and staff resources are pooled to underwrite the cost of planning, each funder pays less for planning. The amount and quality of data upon which to base decisions is greater than it would be if each of the principal parties paid for its own planning.

An occasional agency executive will complain that it is the funding organization's task to raise funds, not plan. This does not represent an undercurrent of dissatisfaction with the evaluations, needs assessment studies, or other products of the integrated planning programs. Recent evaluations of these efforts endorse the program as effective, fair, and useful.

CRUCIAL FACTORS IN GETTING INTEGRATED PLANNING UNDERWAY

There are several factors that appear to be necessary for the successful implementation of integrated human service planning. First, it takes one or two individuals to be willing to spend time over a period of several years on the project. Persistence is a key ingredient in getting any new venture off the ground. In Lincoln and Lancaster County, it was the City-County Human Service Administrator and the Executive Director of United Way. While others have made significant contributions, it was the staying power of these individuals that made it succeed.

Second, without the counsel and active participation of human service agency executives, integrated planning is bound to failure. Their input must be actively sought at every stage of development. Those who chose not to become actively involved must be kept fully informed. This minimizes opposition that could develop on the basis of not being informed or from not having the opportunity to comment. Agency executives must be active participants in the formation of evaluation procedures, priority studies, and other initiatives. In the priority studies, half the members of the committee conducting the study were agency executives. Such representation is essential to the development of a product that will be used and accepted.

Third, it is important to achieve consensus at each stage in the development of an integrated planning program. It is important not to move on to the next stage until serious attempts have been made to deal with every objection and concern raised by the principal parties. New information, compromises, and full deliberation may be needed to deal with each concern raised. This does not mean there has to be unanimity on each step, but it does mean that all but a very small minority must agree that a particular step is the very best course of action under the circumstances. While it means interminable meetings, memos, and consultations, the final product is one that will be used.

Fourth, active input from and coordination with local government officials is crucial. They fund large numbers of programs, service large numbers of people, and, in general, have considerable influence and access to resources. Because of the many competing demands on their time, they did not become as involved in the actual work of establishing an integrated planning program as, say, agency executives. But, they need to be actively consulted at each stage of development and their ideas taken into account.

Finally, there is a whole layer of organizations that do not in themselves provide human services, but have many ties to organizations that do. Voluntary associations like the Junior League, schools, and human service advisory groups need to be incorporated into the development of an integrated planning program. Often their influence is great, and they have a vested interest in the final product.

The system of integrated planning that developed in Lincoln is by no means complete. It continues to evolve and change as the political and social environment change. But that is in the nature of a planning program that is going to continue to be used.

FURTHER READING FOR THE NONSPECIALIST

Benis, Warren G., Kenneth D. Beene, and Robert Chin. *The Planning of Change, 2nd Ed.* New York, Holt, Rinehart, and Winston, Inc., 1969. This classic presents a variety of theories and strategies for social change. Using a case study approach, the authors show the practical applications of these theories to achieve planned change.

Gross, Malvern, J., Jr., and William Warshauer, Jr. *Financial and Accounting Guides for Non-Profit Organizations, 3rd Ed.* New York, John Wiley and Sons, 1979. This is a practical guide for nonprofit managers, especially with respect to fiscal control, accounting, financial reporting to the public, boards of directors, and state and federal entities. Current positions of the American Institute of Certified Public Accountants are also outlined. It is a good mix of theory and practice.

Hatry, H., R. Winnie, and D. Fisk: *Practical Program Evaluation for State and Local Governments.* Washington, Urban Institute, 1981. A guide for the administrator who wants to get started in program evaluation. Suscinct and well written.

Michael, Donald N. *On Learning to Plan and Planning to Learn.* San Francisco, Jossey-Bass, 1973. Michael discusses the social psychological resistences that individuals and organizations have that keep them from doing long-range social planning. The book is more theoretical and philosophical than it is "how to do it," but it gives the reader a sound basis for understanding long-range social planning.

Millan, A., H. Hatry, and M. Ross. *Monitoring the Outcomes of Social Services, Volume 1: Preliminary Suggestions.* Washington, Urban Institute, 1977. An extensive compilation of ways to monitor human service client outcomes. While it is geared to analysis at the state level, there are many practical suggestions that can be applied locally.

United Way of America. *Needs Assessment: A Guide for Planners, Managers and Founders of Health and Human Care Services.* Alexandria, United Way of America. A thorough compilation of ways to assess human service needs. This volume contains many practical suggestions and guidelines.

Weiss, C. *Evaluation Research: Methods for Assessing Program Effectiveness.* Englewood Cliffs, Prentice-Hall, 1972. A primer on program evaluation. Well written, this volume introduces the reader to the fundamentals of evaluation.

Welch, S. and J. Comer. *Quantitative Methods for Public Administration: Techniques and Application.* Homewood, Dorsey, 1983. An introductory volume on applying social science research methods to policy analysis. A thorough treatment that not only covers basics, but reviews such things as cost benefit analysis, linear programming, and decision trees. Designed for the beginner, with plenty of examples.

BIBLIOGRAPHY

Bennis, Warren G., Kenneth D. Benne, and Robert Chin. *The Planning of Change, 2nd Ed.* New York, Holt, Rinehart, and Winston, Inc., 1969.

Booth, A. *Manual for Implementing Follow Up Study of Clients in Drug/Alcohol Treatment Programs: A Method for Assessing Program Effectiveness.* Lincoln, NE, Lincoln-Lancaster County Drug Projects, 1983.

Bureau of Census. *City and County Data Book.* Washington, D.C., 1977.

Columbia University Press. *Foundation Directory.* Any recent year.

Greenhalgh, L. and R. McKersie. Comparative effectiveness of alternative strategies for cutback management. *Public Administration Review,* 4:575–580.

Gross, Malvern J., Jr., and William Warshauer, Jr. *Financial and Accounting Guides for Non-profit Organizations, 3rd Ed.* New York, John Wiley and Sons, 1979.

International City Management Association. *Municipal Year Book.* Washington, D.C., 1982.

Levine, C. More on cutback management: hard questions for hard times. *Public Administration Review,* 3:2–6.

Michael, Donald N. *On Learning to Plan and Planning to Learn.* San Francisco, Jossey-Bass, 1973.

Millar, A., H. Hatry, and M. Ross. *Monitoring the Outcomes of Social Services, Volume 1: Preliminary Suggestions.* Washington, D.C., The Urban Institute, 1977.

United Way of America. *Needs Assessment: A Guide for Planners, Managers, and Founders of Health and Human Care Services.* Alexandria, Virginia, United Way of America, 1982.

United Way of Lincoln and Lancaster County. *Evaluating Human Service Programs: A Manual for Evaluation Team Members.* Lincoln, NE, United Way, 1983.

Van deVall, M. and C. Belas. The utilization of social policy research: an empirical analysis of its structure and functions. Boston, MA, presented at American Sociological Association Meetings, 1979.

INDEX